The G[reat] Reader Handbook

D0570345

collegiate
academy
1999

ANTHONY D. FREDERICKS, Ed.D.

Scott, Foresman and Company

Glenview, Illinois

London

Good Year Books

are available for preschool through grade 12 and for every basic curriculum subject plus many enrichment areas. For more Good Year Books, contact your local bookseller or educational dealer. For a complete catalog with information about other Good Year Books, please write:

Good Year Books
Department GYB
1900 East Lake Avenue
Glenview, Illinois 60025

Copyright © 1988 Scott, Foresman and Company.
All Rights Reserved.
Printed in the United States of America.

ISBN 0-673-18754-3

1112131415 BI 9998979695

No part of the book may be reproduced in any form or by any means, except those portions intended for classroom use, without permission in writing from the publisher.

To Betty Benner — creative genius, talented colleague, and very gifted friend.

Contents

Introduction

"The time has come," the Walrus said,
"To talk of many things:
Of shoes — and ships — and sealing-wax —
Of cabbages — and kings —
And why the sea is boiling hot —
And whether pigs have wings."

Lewis Carroll

Gifted students present a unique challenge to elementary teachers. They are often the first ones done with a reading assignment or those who continually ask for more creative and interesting work. What these students frequently demand are ideas and materials that are not only challenging but relevant as well. What they need are exciting activities, energizing projects, and focused worksheets that offer a creative curriculum within the framework of the regular reading program.

This book has been written with these gifted readers in mind. It contains a wide variety of ideas and suggestions designed to assist gifted children in developing the skills necessary to expand their reading horizons. A major focus of the book is to help children learn and apply the thinking and creative skills appropriate for reading competence. Assignments are offered that both extend the classroom reading program and help students explore the world around them.

Specifically, the objectives of this book are as follows:

1. Students will be involved in a facilitative learning process. They will be encouraged to plan and select assignments that meet their individual needs and interests. In turn, these self-directed explorations will lead to greater personal involvement and participation.
2. Students will learn to assume more responsibility for their own learning. In so doing, they will gain a greater awareness of their own abilities, develop a sense of self-direction, and improve their self-esteem.
3. Students will be exposed to a wide range of materials, assignments, and experiences — all designed to stimulate reading exploration above and beyond the basal text.
4. Divergent thinking skills will be emphasized in concert with creative endeavors. Thus, pupils will be encouraged to both process and interpret information. As a result, they will come to appreciate reading as a multifaceted subject.
5. Students will be able to explore reading beyond the walls of the classroom. By using their skills in practical and meaningful pursuits, they will gain a heightened awareness of their own competencies.

Each of the four units in this book focuses on six thinking skills and four creative extensions. The thinking skills include literal, reorganization, interpretive, evaluation, appreciation, and application. The four creative extensions are fluency, flexibility, originality, and elaboration.

Thinking Skills

1. *Literal*. The literal level of thinking involves the student's ability to locate, identify, recall, and remember specific facts in written material.

2. *Reorganization*. This refers to the ability to sort, group, or classify ideas into new patterns. Putting concepts or items into categories is one method of reorganization.

3. *Interpretive*. Using their own background of experiences, students develop inferences about story information. Making educated guesses is one use of interpretive skills.

4. *Evaluation*. Using a set of established criteria, students make personal judgments about the worth or merit of written material.

5. *Appreciation*. This refers to students' emotional responses to stories or books. It entails identifying affective reactions to written material.

6. *Application*. This skill focuses on students' ability to use information obtained from written sources in a variety of new situations.

Creative Extensions

1. *Fluency*. This is the ability to create a potpourri of ideas or lists of ideas. It involves the generation of many thoughts without regard to quality. Brainstorming is a good way to enhance fluency.

2. *Flexibility*. This skill involves drawing relationships between seemingly unrelated ideas (for example, "How is a rubber band like a dictionary?"). Locating common elements between items helps students look for many possible answers to a problem.

3. *Originality*. This refers to the creation of ideas that are singular and unique — those that are different from all others. It is the creative process we most often associate with gifted youngsters.

4. *Elaboration*. This is the process individuals go through to expand an idea — to enlarge it until it is workable or feasible. It is a process of addition or multiplication that builds ideas into their final form.

The assignments in this book have been developed in concert with varied groups of gifted youngsters. Many children have participated in the development of each worksheet, activity, project, and story energizer, thus ensuring the relevancy of each assignment for all gifted readers. However, it is important that whichever assignments you select for your students, you take sufficient time to discuss the purpose of each one, in terms of both its immediate importance and its long-range implications. Providing opportunities for pupils to share and discuss the implications of these ideas for their own reading development will help them appreciate the selected assignments as a positive extension of their literacy development.

You are also encouraged to solicit follow-up activities from your gifted students. These units are not rigid; they can be modified and expanded as the dynamics of individuals or groups may warrant. When students have opportunities to extend and expand the ideas within each of these units, they will be able to see the value of their work in terms of long-range reading goals.

FROM *THE GIFTED READER HANDBOOK*, COPYRIGHT © 1988 SCOTT, FORESMAN AND COMPANY

In short, the worksheets, projects, activities, and story energizers in this book should serve as launching pads for students' imagination, thinking-skills development, and creativity enhancement.

The assignments are designed to be used in whatever order or sequence you feel to be most appropriate. You should plan to use a mix from the units throughout the year, providing varied opportunities for students to become actively involved in a selection of ideas, themes, and interests. In turn, their interest will be piqued and their motivation ensured.

This book has been written for the teacher who wishes to stimulate, encourage, and extend the learning opportunities for gifted readers. A healthy dose of these assignments within and throughout the reading program can produce pupils who are eager participants in the reading process. In turn, literacy growth can become an exciting and dynamic part of the world of gifted readers.

How to Use This Book

This book can be used in a variety of classrooms, grouping situations, or instructional formats. Here are some possibilities:

1. *The Regular Classroom*. All of the units can be used in a regular classroom containing both gifted and on-level readers. As such, units can be assigned (a) when scheduled reading assignments have been completed, (b) in place of regular assignments, or (c) as supplemental work to strengthen concepts presented in the reading curriculum.

2. *Special Gifted Class*. This book presents a number of options for special gifted classes. These include (a) using the units in addition to the regular reading curriculum, (b) developing a complete reading curriculum for gifted pupils based on these assignments, or (c) scheduling individual or small-group work as an extension of previously learned concepts and skills.

3. *At Home*. Parents will find these assignments appropriate for home use, too. Each unit focuses on a variety of thinking skills and creative extensions, using a nonthreatening format that families can enjoy together. Parents should treat these ideas as fun-to-do assignments rather than as graded work. It is important, therefore, that the atmosphere be low key, relaxed, and informal — enjoyment should be the watchword. Total family involvement will help gifted students apply classroom-learned skills in a variety of practical situations.

This book can be used in a variety of ways, depending on individual classroom dynamics and on the instructional plans you wish to emphasize. In choosing assignments for your gifted students, you may wish to give some thought to the following:

1. Try a variety of grouping strategies. Most of the worksheets, activities, projects, and story energizers can be done as individual or as small-group work. Provide children with a selection of sharing opportunities, too.

FROM *THE GIFTED READER HANDBOOK*, COPYRIGHT © 1988 SCOTT, FORESMAN AND COMPANY

2. All of the units are nongraded. However, you may wish to set up your own evaluation system or have students help in establishing appropriate evaluation criteria. This will ensure maximum pupil involvement — a factor that enhances both cognitive and affective development.

3. There is no set order or sequence to the assignments. You are free to choose appropriate work or allow students a measure of self-selection in determining the assignments they would like to pursue.

4. Whatever worksheets, activities, projects, or story energizers you or your students select, it will be important to keep time limits flexible. Suggested completion times are included in the introduction to each unit but are offered as approximations only. After students have completed several assignments, you will be able to judge appropriate time limits for future work.

5. Most of the units require either some degree of student independence or an extended period of time for completion. Consequently, it is strongly suggested that you schedule periodic conferences with individual pupils or with small groups of students. These conferences can provide you with an opportunity to gauge student progress and discuss issues or concerns specific to individual assignments.

Assignment Scheduling

Following is a suggested plan for assigning individual lessons within each unit. Feel free to modify it according to the dynamics or time limitations of your classes.

1. Introduce an assignment or lesson to individuals or small groups. Be sure to provide a complete list of all the necessary requirements.

2. Have students discuss several options for completing an assignment. Make sure discussion centers on how the assignment will be initiated, pursued, and terminated.

3. Give students plenty of time to examine several assignments thoroughly and to make their own choices. Students may opt to work on specific lessons individually or in small groups.

4. Have students begin working on selected worksheets, activities, projects, or story energizers.

5. Allow students sufficient time to plan culminating projects or presentations. Have them set a target date for completion of a selected assignment.

6. Provide opportunities to share the results of an assignment, to discuss its implications, and to evaluate the product(s).

Reporting Formats

As students complete the individual worksheets, activities, projects, or story energizers, they will want to report their newly discovered information. The following list contains several possibilities for sharing student information with other class members as well as with you. You should encourage students to select a variety of reporting formats throughout the year and throughout the assignments.

book reviews
storytelling
videos
posters
clay models
recordings
chalk talks
advertisements
bulletin boards
dramas
filmstrips
sculptures
games
displays
book jackets
mobiles
drawings
roller movies
murals
scrapbooks
puppets
maps
letters to author
PA announcements
shadowboxes
flannel boards
songs

booklets
illustrated talks
carvings
file boxes
poems
book talks
charts
brochures
scripts
cartoons
folders
guidebooks
pantomimes
panoramas
diaries
reference books
discussion groups
news articles
time lines
dioramas
models
puzzles
dances
collages
worksheets
collections
bookmarks
lists

The variety of instructional options and reporting formats guarantees that students will be able to discover many exciting dimensions to the world of reading. In so doing, they will have the opportunity to use their classroom skills in varied literary explorations beyond the classroom.

FROM *THE GIFTED READER HANDBOOK*, COPYRIGHT © 1988 SCOTT, FORESMAN AND COMPANY

Organizational Chart

This organizational chart provides you with the opportunity to select and assign the worksheets, activities, projects, and story energizers most suitable to the needs of your students. The six thinking skills and four creative extensions are listed across the top of the chart, while each specific assignment is listed down the left side of the chart. You can therefore use the chart to choose assignments that reinforce or extend specific thinking or creative skills. For example, if you wanted to assign an individual worksheet focusing on the thinking skill of appreciation, you could use the chart to select Worksheet 17, 18, 19, or 22. On the other hand, if you wanted to have a group of students focus on the creative extension of elaboration, you could choose Activity 2, 4, 7, 10, 11, 13, or 21.

These options will permit you to integrate the worksheets, activities, projects, and story energizers into your reading curriculum in a quick and convenient manner. In this way you can be assured that your gifted readers will receive the benefits of an all-inclusive and thorough reading program, one designed for their interests and their abilities.

Unit One: Worksheets	Thinking Skills						Creative Extensions			
	LITERAL	REORGANIZATION	INTERPRETIVE	EVALUATION	APPRECIATION	APPLICATION	FLUENCY	FLEXIBILITY	ORIGINALITY	ELABORATION
1. Color My World	●	●					●		●	●
2. Word Whip	●	●					●	●	●	
3. Mixed Up Words	●	●					●		●	●
4. Animal Farm	●	●							●	●
5. Puzzle Me	●	●					●		●	●
6. Crazy Headlines	●		●				●		●	
7. Up, Down, and Across	●					●		●	●	
8. Pyramid Sentences	●					●			●	●
9. Category Fun		●		●			●	●	●	
10. Boxed In		●		●			●		●	●
11. The Right Size		●		●			●		●	●
12. Fantastic Food		●				●	●	●		
13. By Ones and Twos		●				●		●	●	●
14. The Right Place		●				●	●	●		●
15. Making Cents		●				●			●	●
16. Who Said That?			●	●			●		●	
17. Simile Swing			●		●		●	●		●
18. What's That?			●		●			●	●	●
19. What's in a Name?			●		●		●		●	●
20. Word Play			●			●	●			●
21. Word Wizard			●			●	●		●	
22. Character Codes				●	●		●			●
23. More Than One				●		●	●	●		●
24. Hinky Pinkys				●			●	●		●

FROM *THE GIFTED READER HANDBOOK*, COPYRIGHT © 1988 SCOTT, FORESMAN AND COMPANY

Left Table

Unit Two: Activities	Thinking Skills						Creative Extensions			
	LITERAL	REORGANIZATION	INTERPRETIVE	EVALUATION	APPRECIATION	APPLICATION	FLUENCY	FLEXIBILITY	ORIGINALITY	ELABORATION
1. Dictionary Dig	●	●						●		
2. Question and Answer	●		●							●
3. Cross Words	●					●			●	
4. Jack Be Fleet		●	●							●
5. Ha Ha, Hee Hee		●		●					●	
6. Do-It-Yourself Workbooks		●		●			●			
7. Catalog Capers		●		●						●
8. New Labels		●			●				●	
9. In the Cards		●			●				●	
10. …By Its Cover		●			●					●
11. Book Games		●				●		●	●	
12. Book It!		●				●				●
13. Readers Wanted!		●				●				●
14. Advertising Pays			●			●			●	
15. Answer First			●			●	●			
16. Character Sketches			●			●		●		
17. Words and Pictures			●			●				●
18. In The End…			●			●				●
19. Questions First			●			●				●
20. Time After Time				●	●					●
21. On the Spot				●	●					●
22. Come to Your Senses				●	●		●			
23. Ad Campaign				●		●	●	●		
24. Our Town				●		●	●			
25. All the News				●		●			●	

Right Table

Unit Three: Projects	Thinking Skills						Creative Extensions			
	LITERAL	REORGANIZATION	INTERPRETIVE	EVALUATION	APPRECIATION	APPLICATION	FLUENCY	FLEXIBILITY	ORIGINALITY	ELABORATION
1. Books, Books, Books	●	●	●	●	●	●	●			
2. Fabulous Folklore	●	●	●	●	●	●	●		●	●
3. Pet Parade	●	●	●	●	●	●	●	●		
4. Comic Relief	●	●	●	●	●	●	●	●		●
5. Language Lovers	●	●	●	●	●	●	●			●
6. Food Fare	●	●	●	●	●	●	●		●	●
7. Crazy Computers	●	●	●	●	●	●	●		●	●
8. Sports Report	●	●	●	●	●	●	●		●	
9. Name Game	●	●	●	●	●	●			●	●
10. Monsters and Creatures	●	●	●	●	●	●	●	●	●	
11. Bicycle Bonanza	●	●	●	●	●	●	●		●	●

Unit Four: Story Energizers	Thinking Skills						Creative Extensions			
	LITERAL	REORGANIZATION	INTERPRETIVE	EVALUATION	APPRECIATION	APPLICATION	FLUENCY	FLEXIBILITY	ORIGINALITY	ELABORATION
1. Characters	●	●	●	●	●	●	●	●	●	●
2. Settings	●	●	●	●	●	●	●	●	●	●
3. Events	●	●	●	●	●	●	●	●	●	●

FROM *THE GIFTED READER HANDBOOK*, COPYRIGHT © 1988 SCOTT, FORESMAN AND COMPANY

UNIT ONE

Worksheets

*I*ndependent learning has long been a hallmark of gifted-reading instruction. This initial unit offers gifted students a number of motivating worksheets designed to challenge them in a variety of reading areas, to encourage them in the development of both thinking and creative skills, and to provide them with opportunities for individual exploration of selected interest areas.

Each worksheet has two parts. The first part can be reproduced directly from the book and given to students. It emphasizes two thinking skills and is designed to reinforce and extend students' cognitive processes. Although this section can often be completed without additional reference materials, students should be encouraged to engage in extra research whenever necessary, using a multitude of classroom or library resources. This option stimulates students to experience and appreciate the universality of reading in their lives.

The second part of each worksheet consists of two creative extensions that you have the option of assigning. They often necessitate additional time for examination,

preparation, and completion. Many of these creative assignments are long-term, such as maintaining a diary. Thus, it is possible for students to have a variety of endeavors in progress throughout the school year.

Each worksheet should normally be finished in one or two class periods. Each can be completed independently or by a small group of two or three pupils. There is no set order for completion of these worksheets, so you can use them in whatever sequence you desire. In addition, you should work with students to help them select the creative extensions that match their interests or desires.

You may wish to use these worksheets upon completion of a regular reading lesson, as a separate assignment, or as a special homework paper.

In all, these worksheets offer students opportunities to develop thinking and creative reading skills in a fun, interesting, and meaningful format. Sprinkled liberally throughout the reading curriculum, they can add a touch of spice to gifted students' development as well-rounded readers.

Color My World

Directions: Many words and phrases in our language include color words. For example, the word "greenbacks" means dollar bills or money. Locate and write a definition for each of the following colorful words and phrases:

Name _____

Date _____

Directions: For each of the definitions below, locate a colorful word or phrase:

red tape _____

golden rule _____

yellowjacket _____

blacktop _____

blue chip _____

black magic _____

silver lining _____

yellow streak _____

white elephant _____

red alert _____

blackmail _____

silversmith _____

blue bloods _____

whitewash _____

_____ Highest rank in judo

_____ Indian

_____ Place where plants are grown

_____ Girl who visited the three bears

_____ Heated to a very high temperature

_____ Something an expert gardener is said to have

_____ The brain

_____ A novice

_____ A tropical disease

_____ To edit a manuscript

_____ To be sad

_____ Special grass in Kentucky

_____ Laws that prohibit shopping on Sunday

FROM *THE GIFTED READER HANDBOOK*, COPYRIGHT © 1988 SCOTT, FORESMAN AND COMPANY

Color My World

CREATIVE EXTENSIONS

Fluency, Elaboration

1. Find out what a color wheel is. Make a list of all the primary colors and another list of all the secondary colors. Talk to the school's art teacher and ask about the total number of possible color combinations that can be made with primary and secondary colors. Write a "colorful" report and share it with the class.

Originality

2. Do research in the school library and develop a slide show, filmstrip, video production, or photo album that could be used to introduce colors to children in kindergarten. Make arrangements with a kindergarten teacher to share your "production" with his or her class.

FROM *THE GIFTED READER HANDBOOK*, COPYRIGHT © 1988 SCOTT, FORESMAN AND COMPANY

Word Whip

Directions: Find the names of eighteen animals in the puzzle below (words will go across or down). Then write the animal names in the correct spaces at the bottom of the sheet.

Name _____

Date _____

A	E	O	P	C	H	I	C	K	E	N	D
P	H	G	I	R	A	F	F	E	J	Z	U
F	O	O	G	M	R	O	O	S	T	E	R
C	R	O	C	O	D	I	L	E	I	B	T
O	S	S	N	N	U	M	H	B	L	R	H
W	E	E	Y	K	C	A	M	E	L	A	I
L	I	O	N	E	K	E	D	A	A	K	P
Q	R	G	A	Y	S	X	O	R	M	W	P
B	Z	L	A	M	B	C	G	V	A	L	O

Farm Animals   *Zoo Animals*

_____   _____

_____   _____

_____   _____

_____   _____

_____   _____

_____   _____

_____   _____

_____   _____

_____   _____

Word Whip

Flexibility, Originality

1. Create some new animals by taking the first part of the name of one animal and combining it with the last part of the name of another animal. For example: <u>octo</u>pus + gi<u>raffe</u> = octoraffe. Draw a picture of each new animal you create. Make a poster of ten of your new animals to display in the classroom.

Fluency

2. Make lists of animals that live in different countries. For example, what are some animals that live in South American countries that do not live in North American countries? Create special guidebooks to the animals of three or more countries.

FROM *THE GIFTED READER HANDBOOK,* COPYRIGHT © 1988 SCOTT, FORESMAN AND COMPANY

Mixed Up Words

Directions: When the letters of a word can be arranged to form another word, that's called an anagram. For example, the letters in CARE can be rearranged to form the word RACE. For each of the words below, move the letters around to form a new word:

Name _____

Date _____

seat _____

read _____

robe _____

reed _____

spin _____

coast _____

rat _____

oars _____

mate _____

keep _____

star _____

spray _____

net _____

meal _____

span _____

part _____

words _____

bear _____

grab _____

steam _____

trap _____

lane _____

pear _____

lap _____

FROM *THE GIFTED READER HANDBOOK,* COPYRIGHT © 1988 SCOTT, FORESMAN AND COMPANY

7

Mixed Up Words

CREATIVE EXTENSIONS

**Fluency,
Elaboration**

1. Develop an anagram dictionary. Locate words in various magazines or books that are anagrams. Copy them on sheets of paper and provide an illustration for each spelling. Assemble these sheets into a three-ring binder. Add new sheets regularly.

**Originality,
Elaboration**

2. What is the longest anagram you can locate? What is the shortest? Can you create a short sentence that can be used as an anagram?

FROM *THE GIFTED READER HANDBOOK*, COPYRIGHT © 1988 SCOTT, FORESMAN AND COMPANY

Animal Farm

Directions: There are many things to learn about animals. Some important facts include where they live, what their young are called, and the special names of animal mothers and animal groups. Complete the chart below by listing the special features of each animal. The first one has been done for you.

Name _____

Date _____

Animal	Name of young	Name of mother	Where it lives
pig	piglet	sow	pen
elephant			
tiger			
sheep			
horse			
chicken			
swan			
whale			
hare			
deer			

What type of animal lives in each of the following groups?

School _____   Pack _____

Murder _____   Pride _____

Flock _____   Covey _____

Swarm _____   Bed _____

Herd _____   Pod _____

Animal Farm

Originality, Elaboration

1. Conduct some research on a favorite animal. Check out some books from your school or public library. Develop a display or booklet about your selected animal, including where it lives, its habits, what it likes to eat, and how its young grow up. Include photographs or pictures. Create a shadowbox or diorama to accompany your report.

Originality

2. If you have a pet, write an original story about life in your house from your pet's point of view. How would your pet describe its surroundings, where it sleeps, or what it is fed? Be prepared to share your story with others in the class.

FROM *THE GIFTED READER HANDBOOK*, COPYRIGHT © 1988 SCOTT, FORESMAN AND COMPANY

Puzzle Me

Directions: There are many different types of word puzzles. The ones here allow you to use any letters you wish to complete each diagram. But be careful — they're not as easy as they look!

Name ______________________

Date ______________________

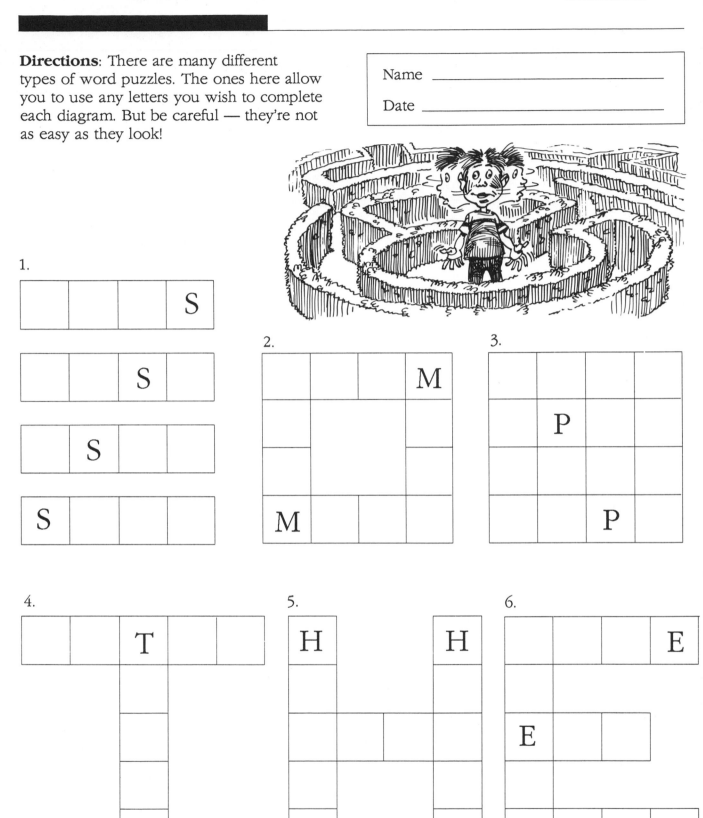

1.

			S
		S	
	S		
S			

2.

			M
M			

3.

	P		
		P	

4.

		T		

5.

H			H

6.

			E
E			
			E

FROM *THE GIFTED READER HANDBOOK*, COPYRIGHT © 1988 SCOTT, FORESMAN AND COMPANY

Puzzle Me

CREATIVE EXTENSIONS

Originality, Elaboration

1. Using the puzzle format from the worksheet, create your own special puzzle. Design it so that specific words from a favorite story are needed to correctly fill in the "blocks." Try to make two or three different puzzles for a single story and share them with your friends.

Fluency

2. Do some research in the school library on the history, types, and variations of word puzzles. Plan to set up a special display in the classroom illustrating your findings. Be sure to provide some sample puzzles for your classmates to work on.

FROM *THE GIFTED READER HANDBOOK*, COPYRIGHT © 1988 SCOTT, FORESMAN AND COMPANY

Crazy Headlines

Directions: The imaginary newspaper headlines below each describe a Mother Goose rhyme. Decipher each one using a dictionary, thesaurus, or Mother Goose treasury.

Name _____

Date _____

1. Nimble Lad Bounds Over Conflagration

_____

2. Jolly Ruler Obtains Necessary Items

_____

3. Azure Youth Found Napping

_____

4. Youth Osculates Unwilling Maidens

_____

5. Children's Group Encircle Solitary Shrub

_____

6. Bovine Clears Earth's Satellite

_____

7. Rodent Ascends Timepiece

_____

8. Royal Experts Face Scrambled Mess

_____

9. Elderly Gentleman Knocked Out During Downpour

_____

10. Youthful Pair Injured on Knoll

_____

11. Maiden Loses Tailless Flock

_____

12. Strange Fruit Discovered in Pastry

_____

13. British Edifice Seen Collapsing

_____

14. Frightful Arachnid Bothers Young Woman

_____

15. Young Sheep Causes Panic at Local School

_____

16. Elderly Housewife and Canine Face Starvation

_____

17. Pastry Maker Hurries to Complete Special Order

_____

Crazy Headlines

Originality

1. Select one of the headlines from the worksheet and create an original story or nursery rhyme based on it. Include familiar people, events, or surroundings from your school or town. Be sure to post it on the bulletin board.

Fluency, Elaboration

2. Survey classmates and friends concerning their favorite books. Make a list of twenty to thirty titles. For each one create a newspaper headline similar to those in the worksheet. Post the headlines and the book titles on the bulletin board in random order. Encourage classmates to match them up.

FROM *THE GIFTED READER HANDBOOK*, COPYRIGHT © 1988 SCOTT, FORESMAN AND COMPANY

Up, Down, and Across

Directions: The name of a popular children's book is hidden in each of the boxes below. With your pencil, begin in the upper left corner and move from letter to letter to trace the answer. You may move up, down, or sideways, but you cannot use a letter more than once or cross your path. Keep in mind that you may not need to use all the letters.

Name _____

Date _____

A	C	E	S	N
L	I	I	D	P
O	W	N	N	A
N	D	E	R	L

S	C	W	H	B	M
N	O	W	I	L	F
T	D	E	T	H	T
H	N	A	R	S	F
E	S	E	N	A	R
P	E	V	D	W	G

T	H	B	I
C	E	T	A
A	N	T	H
T	I	H	E

W	R	E	T	N	G
H	E	E	H	B	E
L	I	W	N	G	R
D	T	H	I	S	A

FROM *THE GIFTED READER HANDBOOK*, COPYRIGHT © 1988 SCOTT, FORESMAN AND COMPANY

15

Up, Down, and Across

CREATIVE EXTENSIONS

Originality

1. Create your own word puzzles using the names of some of your favorite books. You can practice creating puzzles by printing story titles on sheets of graph paper and then transferring the results to sheets of blank paper. Be sure to share your puzzles with your friends.

Flexibility

2. Select a favorite story title and print each letter on an individual index card. Mix the cards up and give them to a friend to put back in the correct order. Ask your friend to make up some cards for you, too. Make up several packets of cards, storing each title in a separate envelope, and keep them handy for others to enjoy.

FROM *THE GIFTED READER HANDBOOK*, COPYRIGHT © 1988 SCOTT, FORESMAN AND COMPANY

Pyramid Sentences

Directions: Sentences can be as long or as short as you wish. In this exercise you will construct a series of sentences, each one word longer than the previous one. Each new sentence must begin with the same letter and must use at least one word from the sentence above it. Here is an example:

Name _____

Date _____

Target word: dogs

> Dogs dig.
> Dangerous dogs dig.
> Delightful dogs dig dirt.
> Dogs digging dirt die daily.

Target word: books

_____
_____
_____
_____

Target word: cats

_____
_____
_____
_____

Target word: teachers

_____
_____
_____
_____

Target word: mothers

_____
_____
_____
_____

MEET ME BY THE SPHINX

FROM *THE GIFTED READER HANDBOOK*, COPYRIGHT © 1988 SCOTT, FORESMAN AND COMPANY

Pyramid Sentences

CREATIVE EXTENSIONS

**Originality,
Elaboration**

1. Find out what "tongue twisters" are. Make a list of some of your favorites. Create some original ones of your own to add to the list. What is the longest one you can create? Which one is the most difficult?

**Originality,
Elaboration**

2. Write a telegram or letter to a friend using as many words as possible that all begin with the same letter. You may also want to try to write a letter using only words that *end* with the same letter. Also, try to write a letter to a friend in which every word begins with a vowel. What kinds of difficulties do you encounter in each of these projects?

FROM *THE GIFTED READER HANDBOOK*, COPYRIGHT © 1988 SCOTT, FORESMAN AND COMPANY

Category Fun

Directions: In each sentence below there is one word that does not belong with the others. Put an **X** over the words that do not belong.

1. Lettuce, tomatoes, radishes, and porkchops can all be used in a salad.

2. Milk, water, grapes, and soda can all be sipped through a straw.

3. Beans, cheese, celery, and corn can be grown in a garden.

4. Butter, jam, popcorn, and jelley can be spread on bread.

5. Cookies, hamburgers, steaks, and hot dogs can be cooked on a grill.

6. Sugar, milk, eggs, and potatoes are all in a birthday cake.

7. Pears, peas, oranges, and walnuts are grown on trees.

8. Cheese, raisins, milk, and butter are dairy products.

9. Spaghetti, ice cream, cake, and pie are good desserts.

10. Pizza, lettuce, ham, and bologna can be used to make sandwiches.

Name _____

Date _____

Directions: Circle "true" or "false" for each statement below.

true false 1. Each of these lives in the sea.
    shark   whale   tuna   lizard

true false 2. You eat these.
    tuna   beef   liver   pork

true false 3. These can be pets.
    monkeys   kittens   rats   snakes

true false 4. These are parts of animals.
    trunk   elbow   chin   pouch

true false 5. These live in a zoo.
    zebras   dinosaurs   pandas   lions

true false 6. These have four legs.
    spider   horse   alligator   mouse

Category Fun

CREATIVE EXTENSIONS

Fluency

1. Make separate lists for each of the following:

  a. Body parts of animals that can also be body parts of humans.
  b. Kinds of meat you can get from two-legged animals.
  c. Sea animals that breathe air.
  d. Foods made from milk.

Flexibility, Originality

2. Create a mobile illustrating both wild and domesticated animals. Use words, pictures, or your own drawings to show examples of each kind of animal. Make a small booklet that shows some of the similarities and some of the differences between these two groups of animals.

FROM *THE GIFTED READER HANDBOOK,* COPYRIGHT © 1988 SCOTT, FORESMAN AND COMPANY

Boxed In

Directions: In what way are the words in each box alike? Underline the statement after each box that tells why.

Name ——————————

Date ——————————

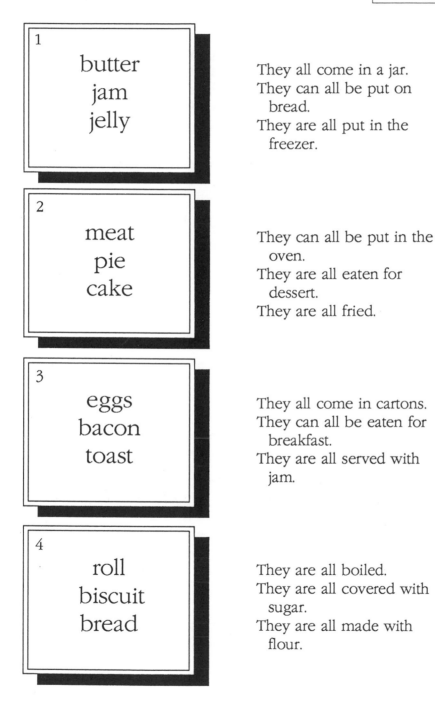

1

**butter
jam
jelly**

They all come in a jar.
They can all be put on
    bread.
They are all put in the
    freezer.

2

**meat
pie
cake**

They can all be put in the
    oven.
They are all eaten for
    dessert.
They are all fried.

3

**eggs
bacon
toast**

They all come in cartons.
They can all be eaten for
    breakfast.
They are all served with
    jam.

4

**roll
biscuit
bread**

They are all boiled.
They are all covered with
    sugar.
They are all made with
    flour.

Boxed In

Fluency

1. Go through your kitchen at home and make a list of the items you find for each of the four major food groups. Prepare a scrapbook about food groups and include a drawing, advertisement (cut out of a magazine), coupon, or actual food label to illustrate each food group. Set up a special place in the classroom to display your scrapbook.

Originality, Elaboration

2. Plan the meals for your family for the next week. Determine what foods will be served, the quantity of each, and how much each will cost. Write out a shopping list and go to the store with your parents to obtain the items. How closely do your cost predictions agree with the final total?

FROM *THE GIFTED READER HANDBOOK*, COPYRIGHT © 1988 SCOTT, FORESMAN AND COMPANY

The Right Size

Directions: One way to think about the meaning of words is to put them in order according to the size of the objects they name. For example, "nickel, shirt, boat, ocean" would be in the correct order because a shirt is bigger than a nickel, a boat is bigger than a shirt, and an ocean is bigger than a boat. Put the following groups of words in the correct order from smallest to largest.

1. house   seed   nail   mouse

2. elephant   dime   toaster   tire

3. lantern   worm   apple   hill

4. elevator   speck   desk   lightbulb

5. cup   automobile   blanket   circus

6. pencil   school   table   book

7. shoe   doughnut   elm   tuba

8. donkey   bee   bird   folder

Name _____

Date _____

Directions: Now put these words in order from biggest item to smallest.

1. sock   ant   octopus   river

2. robot   potato   pearl   squirrel

3. envelope   record   aunt   train

4. jacket   bridge   necklace   chair

5. menu   city   wagon   mayor

6. pocket   porcupine   dictionary   finger

7. postcard   staple   gym   shark

8. calendar   forest   carnation   key

The Right Size

Fluency

1. Make a list of fifteen to twenty different kinds of reading material found in your classroom. Arrange the list in order according to number of words, from those items having the least number of words to those having the most number of words. Would the order change if you organized the list from lightest to heaviest? Why?

Originality, Elaboration

2. Develop a rating scale that ranks the quality of the books in your school library. For example, a 1–5 scale would assign each book a number (5 = super book; 1 = terrible book). Other possible scales could include "A, B, C, D, F" or "+ and –." After you develop your scale, rate books in the library that you have read. Ask the librarian to display your scale, and add to it as you read other books.

FROM *THE GIFTED READER HANDBOOK*, COPYRIGHT © 1988 SCOTT, FORESMAN AND COMPANY

Fantastic Food

Directions: Foods can be put into many categories. On the line in front of each food item below, write the letters of the food categories to which it can belong. The first one has been done for you.

Name _____

Date _____

A. vegetable

B. green

C. fruit

D. red

E. sweet

F. sour

G. grows on trees

H. grows in the ground

I. meat

B,C,D,E,H _____ 1. strawberry

_____ 2. apple

_____ 3. corn

_____ 4. potato

_____ 5. lettuce

_____ 6. lime

_____ 7. tomato

_____ 8. hamburger

_____ 9. ice cream

_____ 10. rice

_____ 11. grapes

_____ 12. ham

_____ 13. celery

_____ 14. peas

_____ 15. pumpkin

_____ 16. walnut

_____ 17. raspberry

_____ 18. chocolate

_____ 19. lemon

_____ 20. peanut

Fantastic Food

Fluency, Flexibility

1. Look through several reference books in the library and make a list of foods grown or eaten in other countries that are not grown or eaten in the United States. What is the most unusual food you can discover? What makes it different from anything else you've eaten?

Fluency, Flexibility

2. Obtain several different kinds of seed packets. What are some of the similarities or differences in the planting directions for different seeds? Make a chart for display in the classroom that tells the planting depth, time to germination, type of soil, space between seeds, space between rows, and time of year to plant for each seed.

FROM *THE GIFTED READER HANDBOOK,* COPYRIGHT © 1988 SCOTT, FORESMAN AND COMPANY

By Ones and Twos

Directions: Many words in our language have the sound of numbers in them. For example: today (two-day). By "adding one" to those "numbers" you can create an *inflated word*. For example: "today" becomes "threeday." For each of the inflated words below, "subtract one" and write the normal spelling. Then put the normal words on a diet by "subtracting one" again and writing the "reduced" word.

Name _____

Date _____

DON'T FIVEGET ME!

Example: sometwo _____ someone _____ somezero

fivek _____ _____

threeword _____ _____

fivetune _____ _____

elevennis _____ _____

twoderful _____ _____

crenine _____ _____

elevension _____ _____

grnine _____ _____

lniner _____ _____

Califivenia _____ _____

Elevennessee _____ _____

tomnineo _____ _____

Directions: Decode the sentences below by subtracting where necessary.

1. Threeday I'm going three the store five a crnine of apples.

_____

2. Twoce upon a time three pirates buried a fivetune of pieces of nine.

_____

3. Threesday was twoderful, except I was lnine five my fiveeign language class.

_____

4. I twoder if the threetor will fiveget the sixteen books about the seventies and eighties.

_____

By Ones and Twos

Flexibility, Elaboration

1. Many words in our language have smaller words inside. Make a special chart listing several of these words and then change them by switching the smaller words to their opposites. For example: "elementary" becomes "elewomentary"; "history" becomes "herstory"; "Illinois" becomes "Wellinois." How many words can you locate, change, and list for your chart? Later you may wish to write a short story using your altered word list and post it on the bulletin board.

Flexibility, Originality

2. Find out what "pig latin" is. Write a story in "pig latin" and post it on the bulletin board. Challenge others to decode your story. Be sure to provide a translation.

FROM *THE GIFTED READER HANDBOOK*, COPYRIGHT © 1988 SCOTT, FORESMAN AND COMPANY

The Right Place

Directions: Learning about the categories or groups that words belong to can be an interesting part of vocabulary work. Look up the following words in the dictionary and write each under one of the proper categories below.

Name ————————————

Date ————————————

kimono	surrey	ark	legume	serape	sapling
sandal	fluid	julep	seltzer	lentil	trapeze
monorail	nectar	snood	yam	conifer	orchid
fern	epaulet	lace	blimp	equine	locomotive
pachyderm	coach	cola	libation	cordial	ornament

Drink It	Wear It	Ride It	Plant It

FROM *THE GIFTED READER HANDBOOK*, COPYRIGHT © 1988 SCOTT, FORESMAN AND COMPANY

29

The Right Place

CREATIVE EXTENSIONS

Flexibility

1. Cut out several headlines from the local newspaper. When you have twenty to thirty, assemble them into several groups. For example, you may want to put one group of headlines into a category labeled "Arrest Them." Another group of headlines could be organized into a collection titled "Elect Them." How many different groups will you need?

Fluency, Elaboration

2. After you have completed reading a story, create a special dictionary that organizes words from the story into several categories similar to those on the worksheet. You will need to decide which words will be important for others to know, as well as the categories you wish to use for the story. Be sure to share your work with others.

FROM *THE GIFTED READER HANDBOOK*, COPYRIGHT © 1988 SCOTT, FORESMAN AND COMPANY

Making Cents

Directions: This exercise is based on a secret code in which each letter of the alphabet has its own price. Based on the costs of each of the words below, try to figure out the code. Then complete the code box in the middle of the page. Afterward, solve the word problems under the box.

Name _____

Date _____

no = 29¢   sky = 55¢   hi = 17¢   yes = 49¢

bad = 7¢   face = 15¢   cat = 24¢   is = 28¢

A =	F =	K =	P =	U =	Z =
B =	G =	L =	Q =	V =	
C =	H =	M =	R =	W =	
D =	I =	N =	S =	X =	
E =	J =	O =	T =	Y =	

What is the price of your first name? _____

What is the price of your last name? _____

What is the most expensive letter in your whole name? _____

What is the price of "oranges"? _____

What is the price of "apples"? _____

Which is cheaper, "cookies" or "candy"? _____

FROM *THE GIFTED READER HANDBOOK*, COPYRIGHT © 1988 SCOTT, FORESMAN AND COMPANY

Making Cents

CREATIVE EXTENSIONS

Flexibility, Originality

1. Find some books on secret codes in your school or public library. Choose a code from one of the books and write a secret message to a classmate. Offer to help him or her decode the message if necessary. Make up a special poster about your favorite code and post it on the bulletin board.

Elaboration

2. Write or describe reasons why codes are important. When are they used and by whom? How did codes get started? What are some traditional kinds of codes? Make a report and share it with other members of the class.

FROM *THE GIFTED READER HANDBOOK*, COPYRIGHT © 1988 SCOTT, FORESMAN AND COMPANY

Who Said That?

Directions: Listed below are some sayings that could have been said by story characters but were not. Match each saying with the character who could have said it.

Name _____

Date _____

1. "I think some dynamite will take care of this house."

2. "I could probably get to Grandma's house faster with a motorcycle."

3. "The next time that spider comes around I'm going to smash him."

4. "If I only had a vacuum cleaner, I could keep this house clean."

5. "If I had more power, I could make it up this hill easily."

6. "I could move into a cave so no one would ever see me."

7. "I think I'll take a little nap."

8. "I like to fly with my friends."

9. "I don't always listen to mother."

10. "The forest is so quiet and yet still full of adventure."

_____ Peter Rabbit

_____ Cinderella

_____ Sleeping Beauty

_____ Red Riding Hood's Wolf

_____ The Ugly Duckling

_____ Bambi

_____ Big Bad Wolf

_____ Little Miss Muffett

_____ The Little Engine

_____ Peter Pan

Who Said That?

CREATIVE EXTENSIONS

**Fluency,
Originality**

1. Make a list of characters from Mother Goose stories. After each one, write a sentence each character might have said but did not. For example: Humpty Dumpty — "I can't think, my brains are all scrambled." You may wish to gather these into a notebook for display in the classroom.

Fluency

2. Talk to twenty-five or more students in at least two other classes at your grade level. Ask them to tell you the names of their favorite nursery rhymes, fables, or Mother Goose stories. Make up a list of the favorites and post it for your classmates.

FROM *THE GIFTED READER HANDBOOK*, COPYRIGHT © 1988 SCOTT, FORESMAN AND COMPANY

Simile Swing

Directions: Many expressions add color and spice to what we read by making comparisons with familiar parts of the world around us. Look up the meaning of the word "simile" and then complete each of the common expressions below with the name of an animal or object.

Funny as a _____

Busy as a _____

Fast as a _____

Cool as a _____

Neat as a _____

Happy as a _____

Sly as a _____

Red as a _____

Sharp as a _____

Strong as a _____

Light as a _____

Proud as a _____

Name _____

Date _____

Directions: Now, create some original expessions of your own using the following sentence stems:

The jet was as loud as _____

_____

The haunted house was as scary as _____

_____

The crowd was as wild as _____

_____

The car was as fast as _____

_____

The clock was as old as _____

_____

Grandfather was as sleepy as _____

_____

FROM *THE GIFTED READER HANDBOOK*, COPYRIGHT © 1988 SCOTT, FORESMAN AND COMPANY

Simile Swing

Fluency,
Elaboration

1. Find some examples of similes in the school library. Compile a list of as many similes as you can. Assemble your list into a special dictionary, providing illustrations for as many examples as possible.

Fluency,
Flexibility

2. Make a list of ten story characters. After each one write the name of an animal that shares a similar personality. For example, after Peter Pan you could write "dove," since they both fly and are kind to those around them. Captain Hook, on the other hand, could be compared to a shark. Be sure to post your list on the bulletin board when you are done.

FROM *THE GIFTED READER HANDBOOK*, COPYRIGHT © 1988 SCOTT, FORESMAN AND COMPANY

What's That?

Directions: There are many popular sayings that people use all the time, such as "It's a tough job but somebody's got to do it" and "Absence makes the heart grow fonder." The following sayings have been altered by substituting synonyms for familiar words. Can you translate them all?

Name _____

Date _____

1. Scintillate, scintillate, celestial object minified.

   _____

   _____

2. Members of an avian species of identical plumage congregate.

   _____

   _____

3. Investigate prior to saltation.

   _____

   _____

4. Refrain from becoming lacrymose over precipitately departed lacteal fluid.

   _____

   _____

5. The stylus is more potent than the claymore.

   _____

   _____

6. It is fruitless to attempt to indoctrinate a superannuated canine with innovative maneuvers.

   _____

   _____

7. Eschew the implement of correction and coddle the scion.

   _____

   _____

8. Where there are visible vapors having their provenance in ignited carbonaceous materials, there is conflagration.

   _____

   _____

9. A plethora of individuals with expertise in culinary techniques vitiates the potable concoction produced by steeping certain comestibles.

   _____

   _____

10. Male cadavers are incapable of yielding any testimony.

    _____

    _____

What's That?

Flexibility, Originality

1. Develop a card game based on synonyms. Using the rules for Old Maid or Go Fish, make up matching sets of synonym cards containing familiar words and unfamiliar synonyms. For example: "best, optimal"; "beauty, pulchritude." You may need to refer to a dictionary or thesaurus for selected words. Encourage other classmates to play the game with you.

Originality, Elaboration

2. Using the format or design for a popular game show, design your own show focusing on word meanings. Decide how many players will be involved in each "episode," how many points will be awarded, the rules and regulations, and how the winner will be determined. With fellow classmates, stage a production of the show for others to enjoy.

FROM *THE GIFTED READER HANDBOOK*, COPYRIGHT © 1988 SCOTT, FORESMAN AND COMPANY

What's in a Name?

Directions: Match the imaginary book titles listed below with their imaginary authors. Put the number of the title in front of its appropriate "author."

Name ——————————————

Date ——————————————

Title	**Author**
1. *The Terrible Day*	___ C. U. Later
2. *Waiting in Line*	___ Ima Hogg
3. *How to Teach Reading*	___ I. M. Sadd
4. *My Favorite Bird*	___ Page Turner
5. *Sprinting Around The Track*	___ Noah Lott
6. *Taking a Trip*	___ C. Howie Runns
7. *Crawling Through the Desert*	___ Willie Makeit
8. *How to Increase Your IQ*	___ Jack O'Diamonds
9. *How to Gain Weight*	___ S. Lois Molassis
10. *Winning at Cards*	___ E. Z. Duzitt
11. *The Mardi Gras*	___ Ima Sparrow
12. *Fifty Years in the Classroom*	___ Newell Leans
14. *Fancy Desserts*	___ N. Struckter
15. *Make a Million Without Working*	___ Pat E. Kaike

Directions: Make up some "authors" for the following titles:

Up in the Mountains ——————————

Learning to Drive ——————————

Furry Animals ——————————

Sailing Made Easy ——————————

Working with Wood ——————————

A Day at the Park ——————————

All about the Library ——————————

Be Physically Fit ——————————

What's in a Name?

CREATIVE EXTENSIONS

**Fluency,
Originality**

1. Make a list of the titles of several of your favorite books or stories. Then use your imagination to create some original "authors" for some of those titles. For example: "Treasure Island by I. M. Rich."

**Originality,
Elaboration**

2. Using some of the fictitious authors listed on the worksheet, create other possible books each could have written. Can you create two new books for each of five different authors? For example: "Page Turner: (1) How to Use the Library, (2) Studying Made Easy." Share your list with a classmate and post your listings on the bulletin board.

FROM *THE GIFTED READER HANDBOOK*, COPYRIGHT © 1988 SCOTT, FORESMAN AND COMPANY

Word Play

Directions: There are many ways to play with words. One way is to write a word in a way that helps define it. Here are some examples:

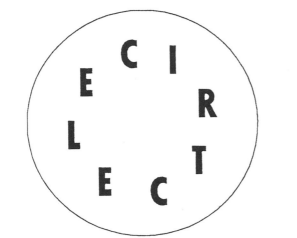

Name ——————————————

Date ——————————————

Write each of the following words in a way that helps others understand (and enjoy) them better. Add some of your own words, too!

mirror	balance	rubber	radio
zoo	lost	pencil	television
race	fast	frown	rectangle

Word Play

CREATIVE EXTENSIONS

**Fluency,
Elaboration**

1. Develop a dictionary of words similar to those in the worksheet. Work with a classmate on different ways to illustrate each word in a way that helps define it. Put your words on sheets of paper and place them in a three-ring binder. Add new words on a regular basis.

Elaboration

2. Select a story character and incorporate the letters of its name into a drawing of the character. Put together a collection of several such drawings and display them on the bulletin board.

FROM *THE GIFTED READER HANDBOOK*, COPYRIGHT © 1988 SCOTT, FORESMAN AND COMPANY

Word Wizard

THINKING SKILLS

INTERPRETIVE,
APPLICATION

Directions: Figure out the word, phrase, or saying represented in each box below. Note the positions of the symbols or words as well as the number of times a certain part is repeated. For example, the solution for the first one is "standing ovation." Can you solve the remaining puzzles?

Name ————————————————

Date ————————————————

O V A T I O N	FROdownNT	MAN BOARD	SCHOOL
PRICE	GROUND GO	ETTR EK RI KC IP IT TP	⌣⌣ ⌣ COUNTER
pAI**N**S	EVERYTHING PIZZA	OHOLENE	T O 2 PAR N
WHAT MUST	LE VEL	MESNACKAL	HEADER HEADER

FROM *THE GIFTED READER HANDBOOK*, COPYRIGHT © 1988 SCOTT, FORESMAN AND COMPANY

43

Word Wizard

CREATIVE EXTENSIONS

Originality

1. Create some word puzzles similar to the ones on the worksheet. Use words or phrases popular with students in your grade. For example, if the term "far out" is used quite often by your friends, it could be illustrated by writing the word "far" outside of a box or house. What other examples can you design?

Fluency, Originality

2. Find out all you can about rebus puzzles. Then develop your own rebus dictionary. Using original illustrations or pictures cut out of old magazines, put together a variety of rebus words. Afterward, create an original short story using as many words from your rebus dictionary as possible.

FROM *THE GIFTED READER HANDBOOK*, COPYRIGHT © 1988 SCOTT, FORESMAN AND COMPANY

Character Codes

Directions: Story characters can be described in many ways. For each of the story characters below, choose descriptive words that use the initials of the character's name. For example:

Name _____

Date _____

<u>R</u>obin <u>H</u>ood = <u>R</u>ascally <u>H</u>ero

Snow White	Curious George	Tom Sawyer	Peter Pan
Amelia Bedelia	Wizard of Oz	Litle Bear	Henry Huggins
Homer Price	Encyclopedia Brown	Peter Rabbit	Paul Bunyan

Directions: The names of story characters can also be developed into poems that describe who they are. For example:

<u>B</u>ig
<u>A</u>ctive
<u>B</u>lubbery
<u>A</u>nticipates
<u>R</u>ocks in a hammock

Here are the names of other story characters. Select three or four and turn them into name poems.

Frances	Charlotte
Arthur	Frederick
Harry	George
Tarzan	Heidi
Madeline	Lyle
Stupids	Mousekin

Character Codes

Elaboration

1. Select two or three people from your class, school, or family. Turn their names into name poems that describe them in some detail. You may wish to make a special poster for each one that includes a poem and a photo or illustration of the person.

Fluency

2. Develop a dictionary of adjectives that can be used to describe people. Be sure to provide a definition for each word and an illustrative sentence. The dictionary can be typed or written on sheets of paper and bound between pieces of cardboard. You may want to display your dictionary in a special place in the classroom and encourage others to refer to it for their writing assignments.

FROM *THE GIFTED READER HANDBOOK*, COPYRIGHT © 1988 SCOTT, FORESMAN AND COMPANY

More Than One

Directions: Many words have more than one meaning. For each word below, write two different ways it could be used or defined. The first one has been done for you.

Name _____

Date _____

Directions: For each set of words below, write one word that is related to both of the other words. The first one has been done for you.

___travel___	fly	insect _____
_____	bat	_____
_____	coat	_____
_____	horn	_____
_____	slip	_____
_____	roll	_____
_____	trip	_____
_____	foot	_____
_____	bark	_____
_____	ring	_____
_____	pen	_____

drama	___play___	game
season	_____	coil
orchestra	_____	gather
flower	_____	ascended
locomotive	_____	exercise
memo	_____	music
carnival	_____	reasonable
weight	_____	hit
shrub	_____	factory
carton	_____	fight
tool	_____	viewed

More Than One

**Fluency,
Elaboration**

1. Several words have many meanings, depending on how they are used in sentences. The word "run" is a good example. Investigate several sources and find out how many different meanings the word "run" has. Make up a special poster that illustrates several of the meanings (you may use sentences, illustrations, or pictures). What other words can you find that have more than twenty meanings? more than ten?

**Fluency,
Flexibility**

2. Find copies of *Rodale's Synonym Finder*, *Roget's Thesaurus*, and *Webster's Dictionary*. Make a chart listing the similarities and differences among these three references. Which one do you think is easiest to use? Why?

FROM *THE GIFTED READER HANDBOOK*, COPYRIGHT © 1988 SCOTT, FORESMAN AND COMPANY

Hinky Pinkys

Directions: A Hinky Pinky is a two-word rhyming definition to a riddle. For example: A "foolish William" is a "silly Billy." Notice that the first word of the rhyming definition is an adjective, while the second one is a noun. Try writing hinky pinkys for each of the following riddles:

1. A fast hen

_____   _____

2. A sneaky boy

_____   _____

3. A small wasp

_____   _____

4. Lemon gelatin

_____   _____

5. A fat cement block

_____   _____

6. A seafood platter

_____   _____

7. A girl from Switzerland

_____   _____

8. A sneaky insect

_____   _____

9. A happy father

_____   _____

10. An honest rabbit

_____   _____

Name _____

Date _____

Directions: Write riddles that could be used for each of the following hinky pinkys. For example: "a fried bride" might be "a cooked newlywed."

1. A shook crook is

_____

2. A cross boss is

_____

3. A dope soap is

_____

4. A dark ark is

_____

5. A flower shower is

_____

6. A blue shoe is

_____

7. A bored board is

_____

8. A fair pair is

_____

9. Nice ice is

_____

10. A dead bed is

_____

Hinky Pinkys

Fluency,
Elaboration

1. Locate a rhyming dictionary in your school or public library. Make a list of some endings that have more than twenty entries. Develop your own rhyming dictionary that can be used by classmates.

Fluency

2. For many years people have tried to think of a word that rhymes with "orange," but so far no one has. Make up a list of words that rhyme with few other words and share it with the rest of the class.

FROM *THE GIFTED READER HANDBOOK*, COPYRIGHT © 1988 SCOTT, FORESMAN AND COMPANY

UNIT TWO
Activities

*G*ifted students need to engage in long-term learning experiences. Such opportunities will help them realize the value of reading as a lifelong skill. The activities in this unit provide a variety of multifaceted assignments, each designed as a separate lesson. With these activities, students have an opportunity to investigate an area of interest for an extended period of time, ensuring maximum involvement and investigation.

Each activity includes both thinking-skills and creative-extension assignments. Initially, you may wish to give the activities to small groups of two to four students. This strategy will provide opportunities for group members to share ideas and options appropriate to completing the activity.

Later, students may want to pursue activities independently and report their discoveries to the rest of the class.

Although there are no time limits for any of these activities, each should take about one to two weeks for completion. Students may elect to do them as an extension of their regular reading program, as extracurricular work, or as assignments to investigate outside of schoolwork.

Integrated with the regular reading curriculum, these activities provide gifted readers with a variety of offerings throughout the year. With the emphasis on self-selection, students can use and extend their reading skills in worthwhile activities that have personal significance and meaning.

Dictionary Dig

THINKING SKILLS

Literal, Reorganization

Ask each student to select a topic of interest, a favorite hobby, or an activity. Then have students look through old magazines for words, phrases, sentences, photos, and illustrations related to the subject area. Tell students to assemble these items into a specially designed scrapbook or notebook. Afterward, these minidictionaries can be set up in various displays around the classroom.

You can vary this activity by directing students to do some research on the history and design of dictionaries. What were some of the first dictionaries, and who created them? How are words selected for dictionaries? How are dictionaries edited and updated? How many different types of dictionaries are there? This portion of the project can be a long-term activity, to include a special display or mural to which additional information can be added periodically.

CREATIVE EXTENSION

Flexibility

Have students create a special dictionary of important vocabulary words found in an individual book or reading selection. What words or definitions are necessary for someone to comprehend concepts in a selected book? Students can create their special dictionaries and display them alongside the books they accompany.

Question and Answer

THINKING SKILLS

Literal, Evaluation

Provide students with several examples of questionnaires and surveys. Direct them to examine each and to make a list of the qualities that are included in a well-designed questionnaire. Afterward, ask students to develop a questionnaire designed to obtain information about people's favorite children's books and favorite book characters. Have students work individually to interview different groups of people, both in and out of the school. For example, students could survey (1) peers, (2) parents and other younger adults, and (3) grandparents and senior citizens, noting any similarities or differences between the responses of three groups. Are there any books or characters that appear on all three lists? Are certain authors more popular in specific age groups?

After students have collected their results, have them prepare a graph or chart to display the findings. You may also wish to have them make up a special report to present to other students. A display could also be created and set up in the school or public library.

CREATIVE EXTENSION

Elaboration

Have students put together a slide program or videotape of their results for presentation to other classes. Their production should contain the results of their survey, photos of some of the books mentioned, plot outlines, and appropriate evaluations of selected books. As other questionnaires or surveys are developed and analyzed, the results can be included in subsequent presentations.

FROM *THE GIFTED READER HANDBOOK*, COPYRIGHT © 1988 SCOTT, FORESMAN AND COMPANY

Cross Words

THINKING SKILLS

Literal, Application

Distribute several examples of crossword puzzles to individuals or small groups of students. Have them practice solving the puzzles, and then ask them to determine the characteristics that go into making a good crossword puzzle. Afterward, have students take the puzzle grid from one of the puzzles they have worked and eliminate all the clues. Direct them to use the grid to create an original crossword puzzle based on words from a popular children's book. They may wish to use character names, descriptions, settings, or events from the story to create their puzzles.

Some students may enjoy developing an original crossword puzzle from scratch. Provide students with graph paper (1" × 1") to get started and ask them to create an original puzzle based on words from a recently read story in the basal text. Upon completion, these puzzles can be made available to students in other classes to solve and enjoy.

CREATIVE EXTENSION

Originality

Show students a variety of other word puzzles (acrostics, anagrams, and so on) and have small groups of pupils create some original puzzles for selected stories in the basal text. To provide examples, you may want to obtain some old puzzle books (yard sales and used book stores are good places to get them) to show to your students.

Jack Be Fleet

THINKING SKILLS

Reorganization, Interpretive

Provide students with opportunities to read several examples of familiar nursery rhymes. Afterward, direct individuals or small groups of students to rewrite selected nursery rhymes from a different point of view, such as to rewrite "Little Miss Muffett" from the spider's point of view, retell the story of Little Bo Peep from a sheep's point of view, or rewrite "Hey Diddle Diddle" from the moon's point of view. After students have completed several of these rewrites, selected stories can be posted on the bulletin board for all to enjoy.

An alternative strategy would be to have students provide new endings to selected nursery rhymes. Colloquial language and familiar settings can be used to alter rhymes with some humorous or unusual results. For example: "Jack be nimble, Jack be quick, Jack jumped over the candlestick, and was given a citation for having an open flame in his house." Or "Jack and Jill went up the hill to fetch a pail of water. But decided to have a picnic instead." It's not important that all lines rhyme in these creations, Rather, the emphasis should be on having fun in creating some original adaptations.

CREATIVE EXTENSION

Elaboration

Small groups of students may wish to dramatize some of their nursery rhyme "rewrites." Encourage pupils to develop a playlet based on their new creations for presentation to a younger group of students or possibly for videotaping. Students should plan some time after the presentation to discuss both the original version and their adaptation with the audience. This activity offers a wonderful opportunity for students to appreciate the various ways a piece of writing can be interpreted.

Ha Ha, Hee Hee

THINKING SKILLS

Reorganization, Evaluation
Ask students to collect various examples of humor. These could include tall tales, puns, one-liners, slapstick, shaggy dog stories, limericks, comic strips, or practical jokes. Students should use a variety of classroom, library, or home resources for their research. Afterward, have students assemble their collections into scrapbooks, with several examples used to illustrate each form. Students may also wish to include a bibliography of selected joke books available in the school library. Have pupils create individual scrapbooks or assemble a large class scrapbook to display their work. Make sure these collections are available to others in the class or school.

CREATIVE EXTENSION

Originality
Have students try their hand at writing a comic strip, joke book, or humorous skit. Ask them to research the elements that make up a humorous presentation and incorporate those elements into their efforts. Be sure to take time to discuss some of the difficulties students encounter in trying to create their own humor.

Do-It-Yourself Workbooks

THINKING SKILLS

Reorganization, Evaluation
Demonstrate the layout and format of several basal reading workbooks. Then direct students to develop a list of some of the features and exercises used in workbooks. You may wish to supplement the basal workbooks with those designed for independent work.

Afterward, ask small groups of students to develop specialized workbooks for some selected stories or children's books. Students should create appropriate exercises and activities that could be used by other students. Initially, you may wish to have students create exercises for some of their favorite books; later, they can create activities for books used by students in other grades. All of the materials and exercises could be duplicated and assembled into notebooks for student use. You may wish to notify colleagues in other grades on the availability of these student-created workbooks and have your students share them with other classes.

CREATIVE EXTENSION

Fluency
After students have had sufficient practice in creating workbooks for children's books and stories, ask them to create workbooks for other types of printed materials as well. For example, workbook exercises could be developed for a newspaper, a travel brochure, a job application form, or a dictionary. The resulting workbooks could then be used for a variety of free-time activities throughout the year.

FROM *THE GIFTED READER HANDBOOK,* COPYRIGHT © 1988 SCOTT, FORESMAN AND COMPANY

Catalog Capers

THINKING SKILLS

Reorganization, Evaluation

Have children obtain several examples of children's book catalogs. Students can get such catalogs from the school librarian or can send away for them from various publishers. When several catalogs have been collected, discuss the format and design of each. What makes one catalog more visually appealing than another? Do individual book descriptions help in deciding whether to buy a particular book?

After students have had an opportunity to look through several catalogs, ask them to create a catalog of selected books in your classroom. Direct them to develop their own classification or cataloging system. To aid in constructing the catalog, provide them with construction paper, blank paper, crayons, markers, and perhaps a typewriter. Ask students to decide on the illustrations and descriptions that will be needed to assist others in selecting books from the catalog. After completion, the catalog can be made a permanent part of the classroom library, with new pages included as new books are added to the room.

CREATIVE EXTENSION

Elaboration

Bring in several general merchandise catalogs (such as Sears or Penneys) and direct students to browse through them. Have pupils select items that should be in the ideal classroom. What types of merchandise or equipment would help create the perfect learning environment for students? Have pupils cut out illustrations of items and develop their own special classroom catalog. Encourage them to defend their choices.

New Labels

THINKING SKILLS

Reorganization, Appreciation

Have students bring in several examples of canned or bottled food, such as peanut butter, canned vegetables, salad dressing, and soups. Ask students to remove the labels from each item (the label and container can each be marked with a special code prior to removal). Direct students to list the type of information found on each label and to determine how much of the label information is important in making a buying decision about that particular product. Afterward, have each student select a product and design a brand new label for it — one that would appeal to a special group of people (for example, children, doctors, people from another country, people on a diet). What information should be included on the new label that would entice someone to purchase the product? Students can display their new labels along with the originals and evaluate the appeal factor of each. It may be necessary for students to set up an evaluation system or checklist of desirable characteristics.

CREATIVE EXTENSION

Originality

Some students may enjoy doing research on advertising. What are some good advertising techniques, and how are they used? Later, students may want to use this information to create "labels" for some books in the classroom or school library. For instance, what qualities should be listed that would encourage someone to read a certain book? Be sure to have students set up a display of selected books with their individually designed labels.

FROM *THE GIFTED READER HANDBOOK,* COPYRIGHT © 1988 SCOTT, FORESMAN AND COMPANY

In the Cards

THINKING SKILLS

Reorganization, Appreciation
Direct students to each select a favorite story character. Have them draw an illustration of the character on the front of a piece of cardboard (or a 3"× 5" index card) and then write biographical data about the character on the reverse of the card. Students may wish to bring in baseball or bubblegum cards to use as examples. Once they have the idea, direct students to create a series of biographical cards for (a) an individual story, (b) a group of stories about a single character or by a selected author, or (c) characters in the basal reader.

Have students develop a classifying system to keep track of the cards as they are developed. Set up a special place in the classroom where the cards can be kept and made available to all students. Prior to reading a story or book, a student will be able to pull appropriate biographical cards from the file and consult them.

CREATIVE EXTENSION

Originality
Using the rules for a popular card game such as Old Maid, have students develop their own game based on the characters in a favorite book or story. Give students freedom to simplify rules or create their own based on the number or kinds of characters in a story.

... By Its Cover

THINKING SKILLS

Reorganization, Appreciation
Direct students to create a series of "shape books." A shape book is made up of blank pages stapled between two sheets of oaktag and then cut into the shape of a popular object. For example, the following titles could be used for books cut into the corresponding shapes:

"All About Me" (shape of a child)
"TV Favorites" (shape of a television set)
"Baseball Stories" (shape of a baseball)
"Autumn Poems" (shape of a leaf)
"Halloween Horror" (shape of a ghost)

Once students have created a variety of shape books, ask them to write an original story inside each one.

One variation would be to have students create shape books based on individual stories in the basal reader. Words, pictures, or headlines could be cut out of old newspapers or magazines and pasted on the pages in each shape book. The shape books could be displayed on the bulletin board or in a special file.

CREATIVE EXTENSION

Elaboration
There are many ways to create self-made books. Have students initiate some research in the library and locate three different ways of making a book. Encourage individuals to try each method and report their results. Which method is easiest? most enjoyable? Be sure students have an opportunity to display their work.

FROM *THE GIFTED READER HANDBOOK,* COPYRIGHT © 1988 SCOTT, FORESMAN AND COMPANY

Book Games

THINKING SKILLS

Reorganization, Application

Discuss with students the qualities that go into a good table game. Have them make lists of the features they enjoy most about some of their favorite games. What qualities make for an enjoyable game?

Next, ask small groups of students to each select a favorite book and turn it into a table game. This task can be aided by having students bring in old or discarded board games from home. Using pieces of construction paper, markers, cardboard squares, and other materials, students can create pieces for a game based on story characters, settings, or events. Students may even wish to set up bonus cards or their own form of money to use with a game.

You can vary this activity by having two separate groups of students each develop a separate game for the same book. Another option would be to have a single group of students create a series of games based on books by a single author. Provide children with opportunities to create a variety of games for various books, and have the games stored in a convenient place in the classroom for all to enjoy.

CREATIVE EXTENSION

Flexibility, Originality

Have students research the history of parlor games. How were they created and why? When did they begin, and what have been some of the more popular games? Direct pupils to construct an appropriate display or mural illustrating both indoor games that were popular 200 years ago and those popular today.

Book It!

THINKING SKILLS

Reorganization, Application

Encourage students to investigate a number of library resources on how they can make their own books. Have them create a special display on the various ways self-made books can be created.

Later, challenge students to create some specialized types of books. The following suggestions may help you get started:

1. Have students do some research on the history and creation of breakfast cereals. Direct them to assemble their information in a book that uses the front and back panels of a cereal box as covers.
2. Have students do a history of their family using a collage of family photographs for the book cover.
3. Trace and cut out a silhouette of each student. Direct students to write a brief autobiography of themselves on sheets of paper cut in the shape of their silhouette. Afterward, assemble all the silhouettes into a large class book.

Encourage students to develop additional ideas for books or book covers that incorporate shapes, designs, or components from the subjects they are writing about.

CREATIVE EXTENSION

Elaboration

Groups of students may wish to establish a bookmaking class for demonstration to other students in the school. The class can be supplemented with a student-designed pamphlet or brochure on how pupils can create their own books. The production of a videotape or slide program could also be a part of this activity.

Readers Wanted!

THINKING SKILLS

Reorganization, Application

Provide students with several examples of job application forms. Have them make a list of the information requested on most of the forms (name, education level, experience, and so on). Ask them whether any information requested is specific to a certain form or to a special job.

Next, ask groups of students to create a special application form for readers. Tell students that they are in charge of a children's book company and that they need to hire some readers for their books. What kind of information should a potential applicant include on an application form? What should the book company president know before hiring the best readers for the job? Direct students to work together in small groups to develop appropriate application forms. Can they develop specialized forms for special types of books (biographies, adventure stories, mysteries)?

One variation of this activity would be to have students create a special application form for potential book authors. What information would a publisher want to know about an author before "hiring" him or her to write a book, particularly a children's book?

CREATIVE EXTENSION

Elaboration

Ask students to interview a variety of adults throughout the school district (custodians, secretaries, teachers, superintendent, cafeteria workers, and so on) about their favorite books or reading material, their experiences in learning to read, or magazines they read frequently. Have

students develop biographies of selected individuals based on reading habits and experiences. These biographies can be collected into a scrapbook to be enjoyed by all.

Advertising Pays

THINKING SKILLS

Interpretive, Application

Bring several classified ads to school to share with students. Plan some time to discuss the more common abbreviations used in various ads. Provide time for students to look through the daily newspaper to select and "decode" several ads.

Next, direct students to create their own classified ad section for a selected book. For example, a "Job Wanted" ad could be created for a story character, a "Homes for Sale" ad could be developed for a character's house, or a "Cars for Sale" ad could be designed for a character's transportation. Students can work together to develop and create a variety of classified ads for a single book. These can then be assembled into a large classified section for display on the bulletin board.

Later, students may wish to create a classified ad section for a group of books by a single author or for a group of books about a single character. Students may want to create "classifieds" for stories in the basal text, too.

CREATIVE EXTENSION

Originality

Have groups of students work with the school librarian to create classified ads for recent library purchases. Students may wish to develop, write, and "publish" a regularly issued newsletter listing some of

FROM *THE GIFTED READER HANDBOOK,* COPYRIGHT © 1988 SCOTT, FORESMAN AND COMPANY

the newest library acquisitions. The newsletter could be distributed throughout the school on a regular basis.

Answer First

THINKING SKILLS

Interpretive, Application
Using the format of the TV game show *Jeopardy*, write a word or group of words on the chalkboard and challenge students to develop twenty original questions that would have that item as the answer. Next, give students a whole list of "answers" to provide questions for. You may wish to keep all the "answers" in a single category, such as "story characters," and have students work individually in developing their lists of questions. Here are some "answers" to get you started:

Clifford
The Wild Things
Tom Sawyer
Laura Ingalls Wilder
Madeline
Amelia Bedelia
Ramona

As an additional challenge to your students, put an "answer" on the chalkboard (selected from a specific subject area) at the beginning of the day. Encourage groups of students to develop as many questions as possible by the end of the day.

CREATIVE EXTENSION

Fluency
Students may want to modify this strategy in smaller groups. Have one student write a list of ten questions, all of which have the same answer. Other students are challenged

to guess the answer within a specified time period. Later, students can generate a smaller number of questions before others determine the correct answer. Direct students to confine their questions to a single subject area.

Character Sketches

THINKING SKILLS

Interpretive, Application
Provide students with several examples of popular magazines, such as *Time, People, Sports Illustrated,* and *Woman's Day*. Have students read several issues of each magazine to get a feel for the editorial content or slant of each. Next, have each student select a favorite storybook character and write three different biographical sketches of that character as they might appear in three different magazines. For examle, how would Snow White be portrayed in *Time, Sports Illustrated,* and *Ms* magazines? Have students discuss the features of each character that would be emphasized in each of the respective magazines.

After students have written their individual character sketches, have them put together a mock-up collection of articles from one selected magazine (for example, *Sports Illustrated* pieces on Rip Van Winkle, Ramona, and Peter Pan). Make sure the mock-ups are displayed in a prominent place for all to enjoy.

CREATIVE EXTENSION

Flexibility
Have students make lists of fictitious article titles (dealing with story characters) that could appear in more than one popular magazine. For example: "How to Escape the Perils of Gardening" (Jack and the

Beanstalk) could appear in magazines such as *Runners World*, *House and Garden*, and *Science Digest*.

Words and Pictures

THINKING SKILLS

Interpretive, Application
Provide students with several examples of wordless picture books. Lead a discussion on how this type of literature is created and how the illustrations convey the plot of the story.

Afterward, have students work individually or in small groups to create some original dialogue or narration for selected picture books. Students may wish to write their stories or record them with a tape recorder. You may want to have students set up a special classroom display featuring a selection of picture books with their accompanying narrations.

Later, have students create their own wordless picture books to exchange with each other. Some pupils may wish to create narration for the picture books developed by their classmates. Have students share the criteria necessary for an effective wordless picture book. Some pupils may want to set up a rating scale for evaluating wordless picture books.

CREATIVE EXTENSION

Originality
Provide students with a selection of news photos (without captions). Ask them to select one photo and create an appropriate story to match the events or incidents depicted in the photo. Encourage students to bring in their own photos from home or to cut pictures from a magazine or newspaper to use for this activity. Some pupils may wish to turn a bulletin board into a large newspaper front page using a collection of photos and corresponding stories.

In the End...

THINKING SKILLS

Interpretive, Application
Provide students with stories cut from old workbooks or discarded storybooks. Before giving the stories to pupils, cut off the last two or three paragraphs of each one, and paste each story on an individual sheet of oaktag. Direct students to write a new ending for each tale. Upon completing this assignment, students may want to compare their endings with the original endings previously removed. Students may wish to attach their own endings to the original stories to create an interesting collection for others to enjoy during free reading time.

Vary this activity by cutting off the last page of old workbook stories and giving the pages to individual students. Ask them to write original stories that would lead up to those final events. Have the sheets bound together to create minibooks for others to enjoy.

CREATIVE EXTENSION

Originality
After students have completed creating several new stories, direct them to develop special-skills worksheets for each story or collection of stories. What skills should be included on these worksheets and why? Later, students may wish to exchange worksheets and the corresponding stories.

FROM *THE GIFTED READER HANDBOOK*, COPYRIGHT © 1988 SCOTT, FORESMAN AND COMPANY

Questions First

THINKING SKILLS

Interpretive, Application

Select a short story from an old workbook or discarded basal text. Record the corresponding questions from that story on a sheet of paper and distribute it to students (you may wish to distribute more than one copy of the questions to more than one student). Ask students to read each set of questions carefully and to develop an appropriate story containing the answers to the questions. Students may elect to tape record their stories or write them. Afterward, have pupils compare their stories with the original stories.

Some students may wish to create their own set of original story questions. These can be duplicated and passed out to other pupils, each of whom can create an original story containing the answers to those questions. All of the stories and questions should be posted on the bulletin board and shared.

CREATIVE EXTENSION

Originality

Encourage students to discuss the qualities of good story questions. What features should story questions have, when are they appropriate to use, and what kind of information should they elicit? Afterward, direct pupils to establish their own rating scale for questions (such as 1–5 or A–F) to rate student, teacher, and text questions. Have students post their scales and use them to evaluate selected story questions used during the discussion of a basal selection.

Time After Time

THINKING SKILLS

Evaluation, Appreciation

Lead a discussion on what a time capsule is and what types of items are normally put into one. Then have students brainstorm about the types of printed materials that should be put into a time capsule. You may want to establish some specifics for the capsule. For example, what types of materials would be put into a time capsule to be dug up twenty years from now? fifty years from now? one hundred years from now? Would the printed materials put into each capsule be the same or different? What items would be put in a capsule to be dug up by children, by adults, or by aliens from another planet? If students could put only ten (or twenty) items in each capsule, which ones would they include?

Have students construct a time capsule using plastic milk jugs or other nonbiodegradable material. Discuss potential printed items that should be placed in the capsule. Direct pupils to place several selected items in the capsule and bury it somewhere on the school grounds (you may need to secure permission). Students may wish to dig up the capsule after a specified length of time (a year, for example) and check the contents. Are there any items they would want to replace in a succeeding capsule?

CREATIVE EXTENSION

Originality

Have students make a report on one of the following topics and present it to the rest of the class: In one hundred years (a) How will reading be taught? (b) What kinds of books will kids enjoy? (c) What will libraries look like? (d) How will books be printed or published?

FROM *THE GIFTED READER HANDBOOK*, COPYRIGHT © 1988 SCOTT, FORESMAN AND COMPANY

On the Spot

THINKING SKILLS

Evaluation, Appreciation

Provide students with opportunities to watch several TV interviews or to read interviews printed in popular magazines. Discuss with them the types of questions typically asked in these interviews and the information obtained from the interviewees. Have students develop a chart of attributes or characteristics needed by good interviewers. What distinguishes a good interviewer from a poor one?

Next direct students to select one of the situations below and write an appropriate interview:

1. An interview between a story character in a book and the book's author.
2. An interview between the student and the author of a book.
3. An interview between two characters in a book.
4. An interview between the student and a character in a book.
5. An interview between the student and a friend about a book.
6. A student interview of an author and one or more book characters.

These interviews can be posted on the bulletin board or developed into playlets for videotaping.

CREATIVE EXTENSION

Elaboration

Students may wish to set up some panel discussions based on the interviews they have written. One student can assume the role of a character, another the role of the author, and another the role of someone who has just read the book. If possible, students may wish to share these interviews with other classes.

Come to Your Senses

THINKING SKILLS

Evaluation, Appreciation

Discuss the five senses (taste, smell, hearing, touch, sight). Ask students to create charts of words that could be listed under each of these sense categories (for example, the taste list might include "bitter," "sweet," and "sour"). Next, have each student select a favorite book or story and locate ten or more story words that could be placed in each of the sense categories. Ask students to defend their placement of selected words. For example, the word "grass" could be placed under smell, touch, or sight.

Later, students may wish to create individual sense booklets of words included in their favorite stories. These booklets could also contain pictures cut from old magazines to illustrate selected words.

CREATIVE EXTENSION

Fluency

Provide several groups of students with rolls of adding machine tape. Direct each group to create a roller box (a shoebox with a "window" cut out of the lid; a roll of adding machine tape is placed on a pencil stuck through the side, and the tape is then rolled past the window and through a slot in the bottom of the box). Have each group record on their tape a collection of sensory words heard or read during a specified time period. Challenge each group to collect as many words as possible to "show" on their roller box.

FROM *THE GIFTED READER HANDBOOK*, COPYRIGHT © 1988 SCOTT, FORESMAN AND COMPANY

Ad Campaign

THINKING SKILLS

Evaluation, Application

Direct students to examine several different types of advertising, both print and nonprint. Have them collect as many different examples of advertising as they can. Discuss with students the qualities that go into an effective advertisement and what makes one advertisement better than another.

Divide students into small teams and ask each team to develop an ad campaign for a book or a series of books about the same character. Direct each group to design at least three different ways of advertising their selected book(s), one of which must be of the nonprint variety (filmstrip, video, slides, and so on). Upon completion, have each group decide on locations or situations in which to conduct their advertising campaigns. Have students set up some criteria by which each campaign can be evaluated and incorporate those criteria into a rating sheet. They may want to have an impartial panel of adults (other teachers, librarian, principal, reading specialist) judge each campaign using the student-created rating sheet.

CREATIVE EXTENSION

Fluency, Flexibility

Have students research various trade publications in education (such as *Horn Book* and *The Reading Teacher*) that regularly carry advertisements for children's books. Direct pupils to make lists of words or phrases that appear frequently in children's book ads. What similarities or differences do they note in the ads? What information in an advertisement would persuade them to purchase a particular book?

Our Town

THINKING SKILLS

Evaluation, Application

Have students work in groups to collect as many different types of printed material about your town as possible. Bulletins, brochures, newspapers, tickets, maps, and other printed materials relevant to your community should be collected from a variety of sites, including (but not limited to) the town hall, banks, stores, malls, the post office, the police station, and the Chamber of Commerce. After a variety of items have been collected, direct students to evaluate them in terms of their usefullness to (1) a new family moving into the area; (2) an elderly couple without children; (3) a single woman; (4) their own family; or (5) a non-English-speaking family. Encourage students to establish their own criteria for evaluating these items.

Later, have students create an all-inclusive brochure or newsletter that incorporates the best features of the printed items they collected. What information about their town should be included for the use of people currently living in the area or those who may move into the town? Students may wish to create their own flyer or a special collage. If possible, make arrangements with the local newspaper to distribute the students' flyer or have the collage displayed in the local bank or post office.

CREATIVE EXTENSION

Fluency

Have students create lists of printed material needed by each of the following individuals: (a) a construction worker, (b) a teenager looking for a job, (c) the owner of a sporting goods store, (d) a homemaker with seven children, and (e) a minister. Have students post their lists in the classroom.

All the News

THINKING SKILLS

Evaluation, Application

Provide groups of students with copies of several popular children's books, and have each group develop a complete newspaper account of the book. For example, have one student in each group work on developing a "front page" for the book, writing up certain story events and giving them appropriate headlines (which events would be the most important to treat as front-page news?). Another student in each group can be assigned the task of selecting several events from a story that would be included on a fashion page (how were some of the characters in the book dressed?). If illustrations are not provided,

can some original ones be drawn? Other students can work on developing selected story events into other newspaper sections, such as Arts & Leisure, Home and Garden, Sports, Local News, Travel, and the like.

After the students have drafted their articles, have them assemble their work into a newspaper. Duplicate the newspaper for each book and distribute it to other students or other classes. The newspapers can also be made available in the library as an enticement for others to read the "newsworthy" books.

CREATIVE EXTENSION

Flexibility

Direct students to go to the public library and find newspapers from different parts of the country. Ask them to look up a single news item and see how it is reported in each of four different newspapers. What similarities or differences do they note?

FROM *THE GIFTED READER HANDBOOK*, COPYRIGHT © 1988 SCOTT, FORESMAN AND COMPANY

Projects

*E*xploring a topic in detail should be an important part of each gifted student's development as a reader. Using a variety of reading skills, a host of reference materials, and a number of reporting formats encourages students to examine given topics from a variety of directions. In addition, extended projects help students develop an appreciation for their own literacy development.

The projects in this section are designed as long-term investigations for individuals or small groups. Each one focuses on a general area of discovery and stimulates the practical application of each of the six major thinking skills and at least two creative extensions. Although no time limit has been established for these projects, each should require several weeks or months, depending on several factors: the amount of class time available each day, whether the projects are used exclusively as schoolwork or are extended into the home or community, class make-up (gifted class versus regular heterogeneous class), and the nature and variety of resource materials available.

Before assigning any project, you should take time to discuss each subsection thoroughly. Students should understand the nature of each subsection, how the information can be gathered or developed, and some possible reporting formats. Initially, you may wish to have students or groups report their discoveries separately for each subsection. Later, students can use a reporting format that includes all subsections of a project.

These projects are appropriate for use throughout the school year. They are practical as long-term investigations that extend and refine necessary reading skills. With them, gifted students can learn to use their cognitive and creative abilities in meaningful "real world" applications.

Books, Books, Books

THINKING SKILLS

Literal
List the steps used in publishing or printing a book commercially.

Reorganization
Compare printing techniques in the 1700s or 1800s with the more modern methods used today. Include costs, time, number of workers needed, and so on.

Interpretive
Design, illustrate, and create a self-made book. Check out some library books on how to make your own book. Be sure to include an original story in your book.

Evaluation
Design and set up a rating system for evaluating children's books. What qualities should a good children's book have?

Appreciation
Write critiques/reviews of three children's books written by different authors. Prepare these reviews for possible publication in the local newspaper. What makes these books outstanding or unacceptable?

Application
Survey people in three different age groups (grandparents, parents, classmates) to determine their favorite children's books. What books are mentioned most and why? What are some of the "classics"? Record and report your results.

CREATIVE EXTENSIONS

Fluency
1. Make a list of (a) all the things you couldn't do if books were to vanish off the face of the earth; (b) ways to compile and record information other than in books; (c) the ten best places to read a book; and (d) the five best books you ever read.

Flexibility
2. Write a report comparing books and computers. What are the similarities? What are the differences?

Fabulous Folklore

THINKING SKILLS

Literal
Compile a booklet listing several American folktales. Include as many sources as possible.

Reorganization
Compile a list of characters from American folktales and their foreign folktale counterparts.

Interpretive
Read several Aesop's fables to some of your classmates. Encourage them to figure out the moral for each one.

Evaluation
Compare folktales that contain animals with human qualities to folktales without animals. Which type is more interesting? Which type is more effective in getting a message across?

Appreciation
Master the dialect from an Uncle Remus story and read it to the class. Do the same for a folktale from another country.

FROM *THE GIFTED READER HANDBOOK*, COPYRIGHT © 1988 SCOTT, FORESMAN AND COMPANY

Application

Investigate several folktales and analyze them in terms of the type of ending they have (happy versus unhappy; resolved versus unresolved).

CREATIVE EXTENSIONS

Fluency

1. Place a world map on the bulletin board. On individual index cards write the titles of twenty to thirty folktales, and pin the cards around the map. Cut lengths of yarn and use each one to connect the country of origin to the card for each tale (pin one end of the yarn to the card and the other end to the apppropriate location on the map).

Elaboration, Originality

2. Write an original tall tale and illustrate it with a "bigger than life" mural to hang on a door or wall.

Pet Parade

THINKING SKILLS

Literal

Make a list of the five most popular breeds of dogs and the five most popular breeds of cats in this country.

Reorganization

What are some of the most popular types of pets in England? How do English tastes in pets compare with the choices of pets in this country?

Interpretive

Write a story from a pet's point of view. What does the pet see during one day? What does it think about? What kinds of things does it like to do?

Evaluation

Survey other students and adults at school about their attitudes toward owning a pet. What are the benefits? What are the drawbacks?

Appreciation

Several organizations provide pets to patients in nursing homes and to people in prisons. Why is this done? What are the results?

Application

Investigate the history, background, and mission of organizations such as the Humane Society and the ASPCA. How did they come into existence, and why do they still exist? Write a letter to your local newspaper telling the community why it should continue to support these organizations.

CREATIVE EXTENSIONS

Originality

1. Write a story about the perfect pet. What would it look like? How would it behave? Where would it live? What would it eat? Would your perfect pet be for the whole family or just for you? Why?

Flexibility, Originality

2. Make a mural illustrating some of the similarities and differences between humans and monkeys. Use both pictures and words, and include as many different examples as possible.

Comic Relief

THINKING SKILLS

Literal
Research the history of comic strips. When was the first strip created and who wrote and drew it?

Reorganization
Compare comic strips of 50 years ago with those in today's newspapers. What differences or similarities do you note?

Interpretive
Dramatize your favorite comic strip. You may wish to create a puppet show or your own original play.

Evaluation
What are the qualities that make a comic strip enjoyable? Do all comic strips have to be funny to be good?

Appreciation
Write critiques of two popular comic strips that have been around for many years. Locate examples of those strips from ten years ago and twenty years ago. Do your critiques still apply? Why or why not?

Application
Write your own comic strip using classmates or family members as some of the characters. Show your strip to other students and adults and record their reactions. What are some of the positive comments? negative comments?

CREATIVE EXTENSIONS

Fluency, Flexibility
1. Create four scrapbooks, each illustrating a different type of comic strip (such as humor, adventure, romance, information). Collect several examples for each category and paste them into the appropriate scrapbook. What are some of the similarities and some of the differences between these categories of comic strips?

Elaboration
2. Most comic strips are published by syndicates. Obtain the addresses of some syndicates and write to them. Ask about the qualities they look for before they decide to publish a comic strip. You may also want to ask about some of the production techniques that are used. Ask them to send you any information or literature about their organization.

Language Lovers

THINKING SKILLS

Literal
Make a list of ten languages spoken throughout the world (each must be spoken in more than one country). Rank order them from most common (the one spoken by the most people) to least common.

Reorganization
Compare different forms of English, such as Old English versus modern English. Make a chart illustrating common words or phrases for each form.

FROM *THE GIFTED READER HANDBOOK*, COPYRIGHT © 1988 SCOTT, FORESMAN AND COMPANY

Interpretive

Ask several students and adults to list favorite slang expressions. Record and count the results. What similarities or differences do you note between the slang expressions of adults and children? Create two dictionaries, one for kids to decipher adult language and one for adults to decipher kids' language.

Evaluation

Many businesses and governments in other countries recommend that their employees know how to read, speak, or write English. Why do you think this would be important?

Appreciation

Invent a nonverbal language (pantomime, signing). Teach your new language to a friend. What difficulties do you encounter in trying to communicate using your new language? What types of words or thoughts are you unable to convert into your language?

Application

Obtain a children's book written in a foreign language, such as Spanish or French. Try to translate it based on the illustrations and the similarity of some words to English words. Talk to a language teacher at the local high school to find out how accurate your translation is.

CREATIVE EXTENSIONS

Flexibility, Elaboration

1. There are many words in the English language that originated in other countries (for example, "curfew" came from France, and "rodeo" came from Mexico). Create a dictionary of words from other languages that have become English words, and report your findings to the class.

Fluency, Flexibility

2. Many words and phrases are specific to certain occupations, hobbies, or technologies. For example, computer talk includes such words as "byte," "baud," "modem," and "disk drive." Make a poster listing four selected occupations and the terminology used by people working in those fields. Are there words common to more than one occupation? Are there words specific to only one field?

Food Fare

THINKING SKILLS

Literal

Look up the four basic food groups. List five examples of food for each group.

Reorganization

Compare the meals served at school with those you eat at home. What types of foods are normally served at each location? Which ones are most nutritious? most enjoyable?

Interpretive

Survey your friends on the types of foods they eat at lunch during the week, including weekends. Make a graph of your findings and send it to the principal or cafeteria manager.

Evaluation

Why is it important for people to eat a balanced diet? What are the consequences of not eating a balanced diet? Share an example from a recent news story.

Appreciation

Work with your parents to plan a weekly menu for the entire family. Write a plan for each meal, making sure all four food groups are included.

Application
Talk to the school cafeteria manager. Investigate the steps needed to plan nutritious meals for all students in the school.

CREATIVE EXTENSIONS

Fluency, Elaboration
1. Make a list of all the foods you normally eat during the week that contain sugar. Make another list of those foods that contain salt. Are there foods you normally eat that have neither sugar nor salt? Make up a menu plan for one day using foods from all four food groups that have neither sugar nor salt. Write to local colleges or government agencies for brochures or information on the hazards of too much salt or sugar in your diet.

Originality
2. What do you think food will look or taste like one hundred years from now? How will it be packaged? How will it be sold? Write a story about your ideas. Be sure to include illustrations.

Crazy Computers

THINKING SKILLS

Literal
Identify some of the earliest examples of computers and the people who invented them.

Reorganization
Compare the very first electronic computer with some of the more popular models today. What differences are there in terms of size, speed, and cost?

Interpretive
What has been the role of computers in schools? in business? What are some of the similarities between business and school applications? What are some of the differences? Survey your classmates and adults outside of school and include their ideas in your report.

Evaluation
Select several educational computer programs. Use each one yourself or obtain reviews of each program from various computer magazines. Which programs have the greatest educational value? As a potential user, what criteria are important to you in deciding on a particular program?

Appreciation
What do you think you would need to know to explain computers to an adult who has never used one? Develop a guidebook for kids to use in explaining computers to their parents.

Application
Talk to several adults and write a report on some of the changes that have come about in our world since the introduction of computers. Do adults feel that our lives are better or worse because of computers? Chart or graph some of your findings.

CREATIVE EXTENSIONS

Fluency, Elaboration
1. Make a list of the features a computer should have before a school decides to purchase one. If you could design the perfect computer for your school, what features would you want it to have? Provide some illustrations of your perfect computer.

FROM *THE GIFTED READER HANDBOOK*, COPYRIGHT © 1988 SCOTT, FORESMAN AND COMPANY

Originality

2. What will be the role of computers in the home in twenty years? in fifty years? Make some predictions on what you would like to have computers do in your home in the future.

Sports Report

THINKING SKILLS

Literal

Make a list of the most popular participatory sports in the United States. Make another list of the most popular spectator sports. Are there any sports that appear on both lists?

Reorganization

What were some of the earliest sports in this country? in Europe? in Latin America? How do they compare with sports commonly played today?

Interpretive

Develop and produce a mock radio broadcast of a well-known sporting event. Be sure to include a pregame show, interviews, and a play-by-play description of the event.

Evaluation

Look through several sports books in the school library and compile a list of some of the greatest sports moments of all time. What factors will help you decide on the most memorable events?

Appreciation

Some high schools across the country are cutting out portions of their sports programs for a variety of reasons. What do you feel are the advantages and disadvantages of a reduced sports program at the high school level? Present your findings and opinions to some administrators in your school or district.

Application

Conduct some research in the library and investigate all the career opportunities in the field of sports. Besides players, what other occupations are connected with the world of sports? Which ones would interest you the most? Design a chart of your findings to post on the bulletin board.

CREATIVE EXTENSIONS

Originality

1. What would be the perfect sport to watch? What would be the perfect sport to participate in? Put on your thinking cap and design your own sport, game, or physical activity for each of these two categories. Provide information on the rules, number of players, timing, equipment, and other conditions.

Fluency, Originality

2. Write a report on the advantages of regular physical exercise for everyone. Make some predictions of what would happen if no one ever exercised.

Name Game

THINKING SKILLS

Literal

Make a list of the ten most common boys' names and the ten most common girls' names.

Reorganization

People's first names come from many sources. Some come from months of the year (April, June) or flowers (Lily, Rose). Other names have religious or historical significance (Rebecca, Jonathan). Make a chart of your classmates' names and try to discover the origin, derivation, or etymology of as many as you can.

Interpretive

Many last names or parts of last names have special meanings. Make a list of some of the more common last names along with their "translations." For example, "Miller" used to mean someone who ground wheat (at a mill). Can you interpret some of your classmates' last names?

Evaluation

Why do you think people often judge others solely on the basis of their first or last name? What would you think about someone named "Butch"? someone named "Gertrude"? Make a report on how people often prejudge others on the basis of their name alone.

Appreciation

Many of the words we use today originally came from a person's name. Examples include "chauvinist," "sandwich," and "watt." How would you feel if your name were made part of the English language? Invent a definition for your name and give two examples of how it might be used.

Application

Several organizations work in the area of etymology. Write to some of them and inquire about the techniques or procedures they use to investigate the origins of family names. Make a mural or poster illustrating your findings.

CREATIVE EXTENSIONS

Flexibility, Elaboration

1. Put a world map on the bulletin board. On separate index cards write the names of classmates, teachers, secretaries, cafeteria workers, and custodians. Use lengths of yarn to connect each card to the country of origin for each name.

Originality, Elaboration

2. Invent nicknames for some of your classmates that highlight their personalities (for example, "Happy" Johnston, "Earnest" Smith). Be sure to focus on the positive qualities of each person.

Monsters and Creatures

THINKING SKILLS

Literal

Make a list of ten creatures or monsters from folklore. Make another list of ten monsters that have appeared in movies or on television.

Reorganization

Describe some of the creatures that are popular in this country. How do they compare with creatures associated with other countries?

Interpretive

Hypothesize what would happen if "Big Foot" or some other creature were captured near your town. Write a short play dramatizing the events.

Evaluation

What do you feel are the characteristics that make one monster or creature scarier than another? Make up a guide that rates monsters according to how scary you think they are. Show it to some classmates to get their opinion.

FROM *THE GIFTED READER HANDBOOK,* COPYRIGHT © 1988 SCOTT, FORESMAN AND COMPANY

Appreciation

There are several groups and organizations that investigate and collect information on creatures that are thought to exist today, such as the Loch Ness Monster and the Abominable Snowman. Write for information from one of these groups and present a report on the activities of the organization.

Application

Many people believe that several strange creatures are alive today (for example, Big Foot, Yeti, the Loch Ness Monster). Choose one of these creatures and investigate its history, background, and sightings. What scientific data are there that the creature actually exists? Make a report, including illustrations, to the rest of the class.

CREATIVE EXTENSIONS

Originality

1. If you were allowed to create your own monster, what would it look like, how would it behave, where would you keep it, what would it eat, and what would it do for you? Write a story about your perfect monster. You may also wish to create your perfect monster out of clay or papier-mâché for a special display.

Flexibility, Originality

2. Design a poster on the theme of "The Most Famous Creatures of All Time." Use both illustrations and words to describe the selected creatures, and provide as many different examples as possible.

Bicycle Bonanza

THINKING SKILLS

Literal

Make a list of the major parts and components of a typical bicycle. Draw a bicycle and label all the parts.

Reorganization

There are many different types of bicycles — road bikes, racing bikes, mountain bikes, tandem bikes, and so on. Choose any two and write a report that compares their various features.

Interpretive

Set up a special exhibit in the classroom on both the history and future of bicycles. What information do you think should be featured in your exhibit?

Evaluation

How does a bicycle rank as an efficient form of transportation? How does it compare with other modes of transportation in terms of cost, maintenance, speed, durability, and design? Survey several people in school to get their reactions, and write a report on your findings.

Appreciation

Select one model of a particular brand of bicycle. Talk to people who own one as well as to salespeople in a bicycle store. Write to the manufacturer for a brochure on your chosen model. Afterward, put together a complete review of the bike that might appear in a biking magazine (you may want to look at reviews of other bikes first).

Application

Analyze the various ways bicycles are used today. Investigate the bicycle's use in exercise, transportation, communication, and sports. Look into its uses for business as well as for pleasure. Prepare a formal report to share with others in the class.

CREATIVE EXTENSIONS

Fluency, Originality

1. If you could put together a bicycle that would have everything you ever wanted on it, what would it look like? What would be its most important features? How much should it cost? How would it be used? Set up a bulletin board display to illustrate your perfect bike.

Originality, Elaboration

2. Look at several issues of a bicycling magazine and analyze the different features, articles, columns, and advertisements that normally appear within its pages. Then develop your own bike magazine to include reviews of friends' bikes, advertisements for necessary equipment, an editorial on bike safety, or other pertinent features. Assemble your "magazine" into a three-ring binder to share with others.

FROM *THE GIFTED READER HANDBOOK,* COPYRIGHT © 1988 SCOTT, FORESMAN AND COMPANY

UNIT FOUR
Story Energizers

*P*roviding gifted students with opportunities to use both thinking and creative skills in a variety of classroom reading assignments can be an important part of their literacy development. The purpose of the worksheets, activities, and projects in this book is to stimulate an active relationship with all printed material, including regular basal reading assignments. In developing this active relationship, gifted youngsters begin to value their participation in all aspects of the reading process, enlarging their reading horizons far beyond the classroom walls.

This unit provides you with a selection of thinking-skills assignments and creative extensions appropriate for any story, book, or basal reader. Organized into three sections — Characters, Settings, and Events — these story energizers can be used to supplement the regularly scheduled reading program. For each section there is a selection of thinking-skills questions that can be asked during the study of a selected story. You may wish to encourage students to pose these questions to each other — an option that also stimulates the generation of additional questions (which can be recorded for later use). The thinking-skills sections also include brief assignments, such as compiling lists. The creative extensions provide selected assignments designed to foster the development of all areas of creative expression.

All the story energizers only scratch the surface of possibilities; students should be encouraged to develop and design their own assignments in keeping with the specifics of individual stories.

FROM *THE GIFTED READER HANDBOOK*, COPYRIGHT © 1988 SCOTT, FORESMAN AND COMPANY

Characters

THINKING SKILLS

Literal

1. Make a list of six words that describe the main character.
2. What were some of the problems or situations the character(s) encountered?
3. Name two events that portray the main character's personality.
4. Name all the characters. List one descriptive word for each.

Reorganization

1. Choose any character. What type of individual is that person/animal/thing?
2. List the characteristics necessary for you to like someone. How do they apply to the story characters?
3. List and describe each of the major characters.
4. Rank order the story characters from most liked to least liked.

Interpretive

1. Which character(s) could be eliminated from the story? Why?
2. How does the main character stand out from the other characters?
3. Do you think your friends would enjoy meeting the main character? Why?

Evaluation

1. If you had been one of the characters, would you have done anything differently? Why?
2. If you could change the behavior of any character, which one would you change? Why?
3. How do you think the main character would like your friends?
4. Compare the main character's personality at the beginning of the story with his/her personality at the end of the story.

Appreciation

1. What were some of the characteristics of the main character that you liked? Which characteristics did you dislike?
2. Would you want to read other books about these characters? Why?
3. Would you like to have one of the characters as a friend? Which one? Why?
4. How would your friends react to the characters in this story?

Application

1. What factors are important in choosing a friend?
2. What are some personality characteristics that you dislike?
3. What would you do if one or more of the characters moved into your neighborhood?
4. Did you learn anything from the main character that would be useful or harmful in your own life?

CREATIVE EXTENSIONS

Fluency

1. Make a list of all the things the characters might say if they came into your classroom.
2. Make a list of classmates who share personality features with one or more characters.
3. Start a collection of items (coins, artifacts, and so on) the main character might have. Construct an appropriate display.
4. Make a costume that the main character might wear. Use old clothes or scraps of material.

FROM *THE GIFTED READER HANDBOOK*, COPYRIGHT © 1988 SCOTT, FORESMAN AND COMPANY

Flexibility

1. Illustrate some of the similarities between two or more characters. Construct a poster with appropriate designs.
2. Cut out pictures of several people from old magazines. Using a combination of body types, faces, and so on, construct a character similar to one in the story.
3. Rewrite a portion of this story with one or more of your friends as the major character(s).
4. Make a three-dimensional model of one of the characters in the story. Use clay, papier-mâché, or another appropriate medium.

Originality

1. Make a sock puppet or stick figure of the main character and act out a portion of the story.
2. Make a cartoon strip using some of the characters from the story.
3. Make a dictionary of descriptive words that could be used for each of the characters. Use words and phrases cut out of old magazines.
4. Cut out a cartoon strip from the Sunday newspaper. Erase the dialogue in the "balloons" and replace it with appropriate dialogue from the story.

Elaboration

1. If you were the author of the story, in what further episodes, events, or discoveries would you have the characters participate?
2. Develop a radio show using some of the characters from the story. You may want to listen to old-time radio shows ("The Green Hornet," "Amos and Andy," and so on) and then develop your own.
3. Write a letter to the author of the story from the viewpoint of one of the characters. What would that character want to say to the author? Would the character feel that he/she was well treated in the story?

Settings

THINKING SKILLS

Literal

1. List all the places where the story occurred.
2. Make a list of six words that describe a setting from the story.
3. Locate the probable location for the story on a map.

Reorganization

1. Draw a map of all the places mentioned in the story.
2. Select and read another story by a different author that takes place in similar surroundings.
3. Compare the setting of this story with (a) your school, (b) your town, or (c) your neighborhood.
4. Illustrate the story location.

Interpretive

1. Why did the author place the story in the location he/she did?
2. Do you feel the setting for this story was real or imaginary? Why?
3. Do you think the story could have taken place in another location? If so, where?

Evaluation

1. Why was the story setting the most appropriate place for this story to occur?
2. Could this story have taken place in your school? your neighborhood? your city? Why or why not?
3. Do you think the author would enjoy writing a story that took place in your hometown? Why?
4. Was the location of this story believable?

FROM *THE GIFTED READER HANDBOOK*, COPYRIGHT © 1988 SCOTT, FORESMAN AND COMPANY

Appreciation

1. Would you want to live in a place similar to the story location?
2. How do you think your parents or friends would react to living in the story setting?
3. Was the author realistic in portraying the location of the story?
4. Describe the setting by writing an original poem.

Application

1. What would you do if your parents decided to move to a place similar to the location of this story?
2. What are some of the important things to consider in selecting a place to live?
3. Survey your friends on places they would like to live. Would any of them want to live in a location similar to the story setting?

CREATIVE EXTENSIONS

Fluency

1. Make a list of six other possible locations for this story.
2. Develop a list of ten descriptive phrases used in the story. After each write the name of a place or town near you that the phrase describes.
3. List all the places in the story that have (a) plants, (b) places to live, (c) electricity, and (d) animals.
4. Take photos of places in your neighborhood similar to those mentioned in the story.

Flexibility

1. Construct a chart listing story locations, important sites in your hometown, and places you have visited. What similarities do you note?

2. Cut out twenty to twenty-five pictures from old magazines or newspapers and construct a scrapbook. Under each picture list a setting from the story and identify it as similar to or different from that portrayed in the picture.
3. Select an illustration from the story and describe how it would feel to live in that setting. Write a letter to a friend explaining what you like or dislike about the setting.

Originality

1. Paint a mural of the scenes in the story. Display it on the bulletin board.
2. Make a diorama of a major setting in the story. Use a shoe box and cardboard figures.
3. Create an advertisement (radio or magazine) for the setting of the book. Induce others to buy property there.

Elaboration

1. Write a continuation of this story with your neighborhood, town, or city as the setting.
2. Plan a trip to the setting of this story. How will you get there, what will you take, and how will you survive? Make a diary of your first week there.
3. Design a travel brochure about the setting of the story. Take photos or draw original illustrations and provide appropriate captions.

Events

THINKING SKILLS

Literal

1. What were some of the most important events in the story? the least important?
2. List six story events in the correct order.
3. Summarize the story in twenty-five words or fewer.

FROM *THE GIFTED READER HANDBOOK,* COPYRIGHT © 1988 SCOTT, FORESMAN AND COMPANY

Reorganization

1. List the characteristics of a good story. Which ones apply to this story?
2. Report the series of events that lead up to the most exciting part of the story.
3. What were the two most important events in the story?
4. Make a time line of the story events.

Interpretive

1. Why did the story end the way it did? What changes would you like to make in the ending?
2. Why did the author write this story?
3. Why would you like or dislike participating in the events of this story?

Evaluation

1. How do you think the following people would react to this story: (a) your parents; (b) your next door neighbor; (c) your brother or sister; (d) your doctor. Write an explanation for your answers.
2. Did you enjoy the way the story began? Why or why not?
3. How did the title compare with the events in the story? Was it appropriate? Why or why not?
4. Was this a believable story?

Appreciation

1. Would an older child enjoy this story? a younger child?
2. Why do you think the author chose to write the story in this manner?
3. Read another story by the same author. Are the events similar? If so, why? If not, why?
4. Do you think the topic of this story is important?
5. Explain what the title means.

Application

1. Compare the events of this story to some events in your own life. How are they similar? How are they different?
2. What would be important for an author to remember when trying to write an interesting story?
3. Do you think there is a lesson to be learned from this story? Why or why not?
4. Did you learn anything new by reading this story?

CREATIVE EXTENSIONS

Fluency

1. Make a list of twenty words that tell something about the story. Afterward, make a corresponding list of twenty synonyms, one for each word on the first list.
2. Tape record (from TV or radio) selected events that could take place within the context of this story.
3. Stick a small branch in a coffee can filled with sand. On each twig tie a small card that illustrates or describes an important story event.

Flexibility

1. Cut out headlines from the newspaper that could be used to describe or identify events in the story. Assemble them into a scrapbook.
2. Locate another story (by a different author) that has events similar to those in this story. Write a report about some of the similarities.
3. Write a newspaper account of the story that would be enjoyed by: (a) a young child in another country; (b) your 107-year-old grandmother; (c) a person lost on a desert island.

FROM *THE GIFTED READER HANDBOOK*, COPYRIGHT © 1988 SCOTT, FORESMAN AND COMPANY

Originality

1. Make a "roll movie" of several events in the story. Using a long strip of adding machine tape, draw a series of important events. Roll the strip onto a pencil and show it to a friend.
2. Dramatize the story in a play or skit.
3. Write an original song (using a popular tune) for the story events.
4. Create a crossword puzzle based on the story.

Elaboration

1. Develop a pantomime about the events in the story. Draft a continuation of the story and share it through pantomime.
2. Create a wordless picture book that illustrates the important events of the story. Create an original cover, too.
3. Create a reference guide for the story. Combine the elements of a dictionary, thesaurus, atlas, biographical dictionary, Who's Who, and an almanac into a booklet that would help others understand or appreciate the story.

FROM *THE GIFTED READER HANDBOOK*, COPYRIGHT © 1988 SCOTT, FORESMAN AND COMPANY

Answer Key for Unit One: Worksheets

Color My World (p. 3)

red tape: complicated official routine
golden rule: treat others as you would have them
  treat you
yellowjacket: stinging insect
blacktop: highway or road covering
blue chip: high-quality stock
black magic: witchcraft
silver lining: the good part of a bad situation
yellow streak: cowardice
white elephant: a useless possession
red alert: high-priority emergency
blackmail: obtaining payment on the basis of threats
silversmith: one who works with silver
blue bloods: members of socially prominent families
whitewash: to cover up
black belt: highest rank in judo
red man: Indian
greenhouse: place where plants are grown
Goldilocks: girl who visited the three bears
red hot: heated to a very high temperature
green thumb: something an expert gardener is said to
  have
gray matter: the brain
greenhorn: a novice
yellow fever: a tropical disease
blue pencil: to edit a manuscript
blue: to be sad
bluegrass: special grass in Kentucky
blue laws: laws that prohibit shopping on Sunday

Word Whip (p. 5)

Farm Animals	Zoo Animals
chicken	giraffe
rooster	crocodile
lamb	camel
cow	lion
horse	monkey
goose	bear
pig	llama
duck	zebra
dog	hippo

Mixed Up Words (p. 7)

seat — eats
read — dear
robe — bore
reed — deer
spin — nips
coast — coats
rat — tar
oars — soar
mate — tame
keep — peek
star — rats
spray — prays

net — ten
meal — lame
span — pans
part — trap
words — sword
bear — bare
grab — brag
steam — meats
trap — part
lane — lean
pear — reap
lap — pal

Animal Farm (p. 9)

elephant: calf — cow — jungle/cage
tiger: cub — tigress — lair
sheep: lamb — ewe — fold/pen
horse: colt — mare — stable
chicken: chick/peep — hen — coop
swan: cygnet — pen — lake
whale: calf — cow — ocean
hare: leveret — doe — hole
deer: fawn — doe — forest

school: fish
murder: crows
flock: geese (or other birds)
swarm: bees
herd: cows (sheep, other hooved animals)
pack: wolves
pride: lions
covey: quail
bed: oysters
pod: whales

FROM *THE GIFTED READER HANDBOOK*, COPYRIGHT © 1988 SCOTT, FORESMAN AND COMPANY

Crazy Headlines *(p. 13)*

1. Jack Be Nimble, Jack Be Quick
2. Old King Cole
3. Little Boy Blue
4. Georgie, Porgie, Pudding and Pie
5. Ring Around the Mulberry Bush
6. The Cat and the Fiddle
7. Hickory Dickory Dock
8. Humpty Dumpty
9. It's Raining, It's Pouring
10. Jack and Jill
11. Little Bo-Peep
12. Little Jack Horner
13. London Bridge Is Falling Down
14. Little Miss Muffett
15. Mary Had a Little Lamb
16. Old Mother Hubbard
17. Pat-a-Cake

Up, Down, and Across *(p. 15)*

Alice in Wonderland
The Cat in the Hat
Where the Wild Things Are
Snow White and the Seven Dwarfs

Category Fun *(p. 19)*

1. porkchops
2. grapes
3. cheese
4. popcorn
5. cookies
6. potatoes
7. peas
8. raisins
9. spaghetti
10. pizza

1. false
2. true
3. true
4. true
5. false
6. false

Boxed In *(p. 21)*

1. They can all be put on bread.
2. They can all be put in the oven.
3. They can all be eaten for breakfast.
4. They are all made with flour.

The Right Size *(p. 23)*

1. seed, nail, mouse, house
2. dime, toaster, tire, elephant
3. worm, apple, lantern, hill
4. speck, lightbulb, desk, elevator
5. cup, blanket, automobile, circus
6. pencil, book, table, school
7. doughnut, shoe, tuba, elm
8. bee, bird, folder, donkey

1. river, octopus, sock, ant
2. robot, squirrel, potato, pearl
3. train, aunt, record, envelope
4. bridge, chair, jacket, necklace
5. city, mayor, wagon, menu
6. porcupine, dictionary, pocket, finger
7. gym, shark, postcard, staple
8. forest, calendar, carnation, key

Fantastic Food *(p. 25)*

1. B, C, D, E, H
2. B, C, D, E, F, G
3. A, B, E, H
4. A, H
5. A, B, H
6. B, C, F, G
7. B, C, D, H
8. I
9. B, C, D, E
10. A, H
11. B, C, D, E, F, H
12. D, I
13. A, B, H
14. A, B, E, H
15. A, B, H
16. B, G
17. B, C, D, E, H
18. E
19. B, C, F, G
20. A, B, H

By Ones and Twos *(p. 27)*

fivek — fork — threek
threeword — toward — oneward
fivetune — fortune — threetune
elevennis — tennis — nineis
twoderful — wonderful — zeroderful
crenine — create — creseven
elevension — tension — ninesion
grning — great — grseven
lniner — later — lsevener
Califivenia — California — Calithreenia
Elevennessee — Tennessee — Ninenessee
Tomnineo — Tomato — Tomseveno

FROM *THE GIFTED READER HANDBOOK*, COPYRIGHT © 1988 SCOTT, FORESMAN AND COMPANY

1. Today I'm going to the store for a crate of apples.
2. Once upon a time two pirates buried a fortune of pieces of eight.
3. Tuesday was wonderful, except I was late for my foreign language class.
4. I wonder if the tutor will forget the fifteen books about the sixties and seventies.

The Right Place (p. 29)

Drink It	Wear It
fluid	kimono
nectar	sandal
julep	epaulet
cola	snood
seltzer	lace
libation	serape
cordial	ornament

Ride It	Plant It
monorail	fern
pachyderm	legume
surrey	yam
coach	lentil
ark	conifer
blimp	sapling
equine	orchid
trapeze	
locomotive	

Making Cents (p. 31)

A = 1¢, B = 2¢, C = 3¢, etc.

Who Said That? (p. 33)

1. Big Bad Wolf
2. Red Riding Hood's Wolf
3. Little Miss Muffett
4. Cinderella
5. The Little Engine
6. The Ugly Duckling
7. Sleeping Beauty
8. Peter Pan
9. Peter Rabbit
10. Bambi

What's That? (p. 37)

1. Twinkle, twinkle little star.
2. Birds of a feather flock together.
3. Look before you leap.
4. Don't cry over spilt milk.
5. The pen is mightier than the sword.
6. You can't teach an old dog new tricks.
7. Spare the rod and spoil the child.
8. Where there's smoke, there's fire.
9. Too many cooks spoil the soup.
10. Dead men tell no tales.

What's in a Name? (p. 39)

1. I. M. Sadd
2. S. Lois Molassis
3. Page Turner
4. Ima Sparrow
5. C. Howie Runns
6. C. U. Later
7. Willie Makeit
8. Noah Lott
9. Ima Hogg
10. Jack O'Diamonds
11. Newell Leans
12. N. Struckter
13. Pat E. Kaike
14. E. Z. Duzitt

Word Wizard (p. 43)

standing ovation
down in front
man overboard
high school
the right price
go underground
round trip ticket
check out counter
growing pains
pizza with everything on it
a hole in one
not up to par
what goes up must come down
split level
between meal snack
double header

FROM *THE GIFTED READER HANDBOOK*, COPYRIGHT © 1988 SCOTT, FORESMAN AND COMPANY

More Than One (p. 47)

bat: animal, stick
coat: clothing, cover
horn: instrument, animal part
slip: trip, clothing
roll: bread, rock
trip: fall, journey
foot: body part, bottom
bark: dog sound, tree part
ring: jewelry, sound
pen: enclosure, writing tool

spring
band
rose
train
note
fair
pound
plant
box
saw

Hinky Pinkys (p. 49)

1. quick chick
2. sly guy
3. wee bee
4. yellow jello
5. thick brick
6. fish dish
7. Swiss miss
8. sly fly
9. glad dad
10. fair hare

1. an upset thief
2. an angry employer
3. a stupid cleanser
4. a boat with no lights
5. a plant rainstorm
6. tinted footwear
7. an unhappy piece of wood
8. honest twins
9. delightful frozen water
10. a piece of furniture without life

FROM *THE GIFTED READER HANDBOOK*, COPYRIGHT © 1988 SCOTT, FORESMAN AND COMPANY